THINGS YOUR MOTHER NEVER TAUGHT YOU VOLUME II

Charlotte Slater

Artwork by Detroit News staff artist
RICHARD R. RINKE

AN ALLIGATOR BOOK

SHEED AND WARD, INC.

Subsidiary of Universal Press Syndicate

Library of Congress Card Number 74-1540

ISBN: 0-8362-0576-6

HOW-TO-DO-IT-INDEX

HERE'S HOW TO:

Things Your Mother Never Taught You

When Charlotte Slater began writing a fix-it advice column for the Detroit NEWS, she brought—in terms of mechanical experience—nothing to aid her.

In fact, she says, "I was chosen to do this column because I know absolutely nothing about mechanical repairs. The idea was that I, as a dummy in these matters, could explain basics to other dummies once I found out how to do a particular job.

"The result is that I started from scratch on each column, seeking advice from professionals in whatever field. If I don't feel I have a solid understanding of a project, I don't write it."

This second volume covers 45 basic household and automotive fix-it jobs. It is a handbook to liberate women from the tyranny of waiting—for a husband to make repairs on the weekend (between games on TV)—waiting for the plumber, or electrician, to come by sometime next week—waiting for the bill.

The Detroit NEWS created this how-to-fix-it service a year ago. The feature now appears weekly in over 150 newspapers in the United States and Canada.

1/ Check car oil

Learning to check the oil in your own car can be a handy thing, with gas stations closed so often and busy when they are open.

There is a rod called a dipstick that extends into your car's crankcase or oil pan and is made expressly for measuring the oil level. It has marks on the end of it to indicate whether the oil level is satisfactory or running low.

You can find two dipsticks on your engine if you have an automatic transmission. One dipstick is for oil and the other for transmission fluid.

How do you tell them apart? The one for the transmission is located on the passenger side of the engine way back near the dashboard. The oil dipstick can be located almost anywhere else on the engine—the sides, front or top—anyplace the transmission stick isn't.

Look for a hefty wire handle curved into a loop at the end (see sketch). There isn't anything else that looks like a dipstick, so you shouldn't get confused.

Turn the car engine off before checking your oil and let it sit for two or three minutes while the oil settles down. In fact, first thing in the morning, before you start the car is the best time to check the

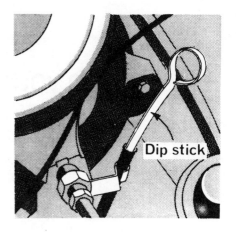

Dip stick

7

oil level. If you check while the motor is running, the oil is sloshing around and you won't get an accurate reading.

Pull the dipstick out of its little slot and wipe it clean. Now reinsert it, making sure you poke it in as far as it will go.

Pull it out once more and note the level of the oil film on the stick. There will be a mark on the stick designating "full." Another mark will indicate the level at which one quart should be added.

If the oil is at the "add one" mark, one quart should bring it up to "full" again. It's not good for the engine to overfill it with oil. So if your oil level is somewhere between "full" and "add one," let it go until it needs a whole quart.

If there is no oil film at all on the dipstick, you're in trouble and need two quarts or more. (The oil light on your dashboard should also warn you if you get dangerously low like that.)

After checking the oil, put the dipstick back where it belongs, seating if firmly.

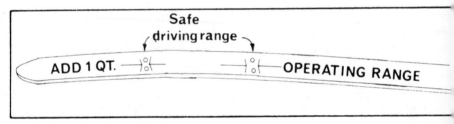

HERE'S HOW TO:

2/ Replenish your car's oil

It is possible to save a third to a half the cost of motor oil by putting it in your car yourself instead of having it done at a gas station.

The auto supply sections of department and discount stores usu-ally carry motor oil—their own brands and standard commercial brands. The price per quart is significantly lower than in a station; and if you buy the oil by the case, it is lower yet.

You can also buy one of those spouts to stick into the top of the can (like the ones used in gas stations) for under a dollar. But a "church key" can opener and a kitchen funnel will do just as well.

Oil is essential to keep your car engine from literally burning itself up. It coats the moving parts in the engine to reduce friction.

Motor oil comes in various "weights" or viscosities. The owner's manual for your car should list the weight recommended for your particular model. If not, check with the person who services your car most often to find out what is used.

Once you have determined by checking the dipstick that the car is low on oil, you will be adding one quart—two quarts in extreme cases.

The hole into which you pour the oil is usually to be found somewhere on the valve cover of the engine.

The valve cover is a long section of metal, rectangular with rounded edges, that runs from the front to the back of the engine (see sketch). Eight-cylinder engines have two valve covers—one on each side of the engine. Six-cylinder engines have only one valve cover.

With an eight-cylinder engine, one of the valve covers is usually hooked with hoses and other paraphernalia to the air cleaner (the round thing that sits up on top of the engine and looks like part of a vacuum cleaner). The other valve

cover (the one on the opposite side of the engine) is usually relatively free of encumbrances. Look on this one for the oil cap.

The oil cap is usually a fairly flat cap about the size of a silver dollar with little wings sticking out from it (see sketch). It comes off easily when you give it a half turn counterclockwise.

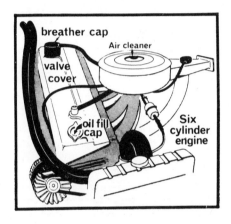

A six-cylinder engine often has the same type of cap toward the front of its single valve cover. If so, that's the opening you want.

But if you don't see such a cap, yours may be the type of engine with a removable "breather cap" for adding oil. The breather cap connects the valve cover with the air cleaner. Some engines have a separate breather cap and oil cap. Some combine the two functions in the breather cap.

The breather cap is round, black and about three inches tall. It sits on top of the valve cover, as shown in the accompanying sketch.

If it doubles as an oil cap, it will probably be closer to the front of the engine than the one shown in the sketch; and there will be no flat, winged oil cap.

Give it a quarter turn counterclockwise and pull up. If it is stubborn, turn it back and forth a couple of times and put one finger under the hose connection to give added grip as you pull up. Do not, however, pull on the hose itself.

But the best possible piece of advice is this: Pouring oil into the wrong hole could be disastrous. So if your engine does not match any of these descriptions or if there is doubt in your mind about what you are doing, get out of your car and watch the attendant the next time you have the gas station add oil to your engine.

One assumes he will be putting it in the right place. Once you see it done, you'll be able to do the chore yourself from then on.

3/ Unstick that stubborn choke

In cold or wet weather it's not uncommon to hear a car grind and grind trying to start. The battery seems fine, but the engine just won't catch—it sounds almost like it's flooded.

This condition is often caused by a sticking automatic choke valve. A simple procedure involving a screwdriver will usually get the car started.

If the cause of the sluggish start is something other than the choke, you won't harm the car—and you won't lose anything except about five minutes by trying the screwdriver trick.

The first thing to remember is not to grind the starter forever. If the engine does not start, do not hold the key in the start position for more than about 30 seconds. To do so is to risk overheating the starter.

Now to the choke valve. It is a "butterfly" disc that opens and closes to keep the right blend of fuel and air going to the engine. It can be found under the air cleaner lid.

The air cleaner is a large circular metal thing sitting up on top of the engine. It looks like it could be part of a vacuum cleaner (see sketch A).

Take the top off of it by turning the small wing nut you should find in the middle of the lid (sketch A). The body of the air cleaner surrounds the choke valve mechanism. With the lid removed, you should be able to peer down the center of the air cleaner and see the choke valve—a round or rectangular disc that flips when you poke it (see cutaway sketch B).

The valve itself is split by a hinge and one side of the disc is usually larger than the other.

Take a screwdriver with a fat handle and a blade no longer than about 6 inches. Insert the blade of it into the choke valve to hold the choke open. If possible, flip the smaller section of the valve upward and insert the screwdriver blade there (see sketch B).

Choosing the small side is a protection against the screwdriver falling through the opening down into the engine. (You use a screwdriver with a fat handle for the same reason.)

Leaving the screwdriver in place, start the car. If you had been grinding the starter for awhile before inserting the screwdriver, your engine may be flooded. If so, push the accelerator all the way to the floor and hold it there while you try to start the car. You can leave the screwdriver in place for a couple of minutes while the car warms up, too. But, naturally, remove the screwdriver and replace the air cleaner lid before you drive anywhere.

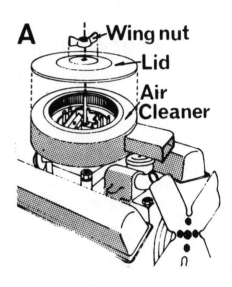

A **Wing nut** **Lid** **Air Cleaner**

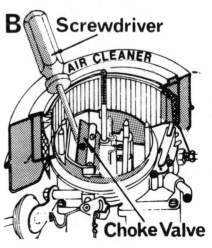

B **Screwdriver** AIR CLEANER **Choke Valve**

4/ Replace windshield wipers

Why give yourself a crick in the neck peering between the streaks on your car's windshield?

Windshield wiper blades are simple to change. You can keep a supply on hand. And whenever road oil, salt spray and sun have sent your wiper blades to that big junkyard in the sky, you can replace them yourself.

Two types are among the most common. One is held in place by two small metal arches with red buttons on them (sketch A); the other is attached to one long metal arch with no buttons on it (sketch B). Both styles come in varying lengths. So find out what size your car takes before stocking up at a gas station or auto supply store.

We'll take the kind with the red buttons first.

The two small arches disconnect from the straight support bar on the wiper arm. But you really only need to remove one of them (it doesn't make any difference which one). On some models you will find a button on only one of the arches; the button might even be black. But don't be alarmed, the procedure is basically the same.

Pick your arch. Press down on that arch's little red button. Pull the arch down and away from the end of the straight support bar while continuing to press the red button (see sketch A). If one span won't turn loose for you, try the other one.

Each arch grips the spine of the wiper blade with small, turned-under prongs. Slide the old blade lengthwise out of the prongs.

In looking at the new blade, you will see that the spine of it is reinforced with a strip of metal. The prongs on the metal arches fit around the metal reinforcing strip, as shown in sketch A.

Slip the new blade into the arch that is still attached to the wiper arm. Now slip the detached arch over the free end of the new wiper blade. Don't slip the arch on backward. One end of the arched piece

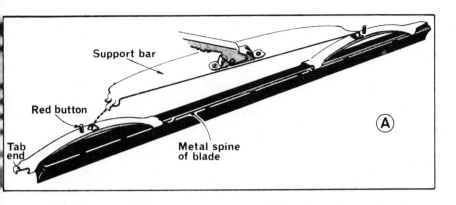

Support bar

Red button

Tab end

Metal spine of blade

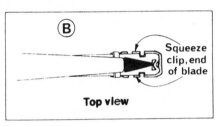

Squeeze clip, end of blade

Top view

has a little turned-down tab that fits over the end of the wiper blade (see sketch A).

Now connect the free arch back to the end of the straight support bar. Just insert the prong on the end of the support bar into the hole next to the red button on the arched piece and press together until you hear a click. (On one-button models, two prongs on the support bar fit into corresponding slots on the arched piece. Just press the prongs into the slots until they click into place.

The other style of windshield wiper blade (without the red buttons) is a bit easier to describe (although both styles are easy to change).

There is only one thing you need to pinch, poke or otherwise mangle—and that is the very end of the wiper blade. You will see that one end has a metal clip that is slightly wider and sticks out a little

farther than the other end of the blade.

Squeeze in on the sides of the clip (see sketch B). The edges are sharp, so use a small pair of pliers if you wish. This releases two little notches from the grip of the prongs at the end of the blade arm. Then just slide the blade out (it is held by prongs wrapped around its spine, just as in the other case).

Slide the new blade into place until the prongs at the end of the arm snap over the notches at the end of the new blade. Take it slow and easy or you will push the new blade in too far—past the notches at the end. If you do you may have a hard time getting it out again.

5/ Start your car on wet days

Damp, misty, or rainy days can be almost as bad as cold days for starting a car. If yours is recalcitrant, there are several tricks to try—one of which is wiping moisture from the distributor cap, coil and spark plug connections.

This is a reasonably simple operation that boils down to one principle: Clean what you can reach with ease. If you can't find it, forget it.

The distributor cap, coil and spark plugs are part of the electrical system of the car. So turn off the ignition.

It doesn't matter if you don't know what coils or spark plugs look like. Key in on the distributor cap. It is located in different places on different cars. But it is easy to spot because it is about the size of a small can of shortening and is the only thing in the engine that looks like an octopus (see sketch).

A main wire comes out from the center of the distributor cap top. It is surrounded by four or six or eight smaller wires. All detach from the cap with a twist and steady pull.

But do not pull on the wire itself. It is held in place on the cap with a rubber "boot" (see sketch). Grasp each wire by its boot when removing it.

And never remove all the wires at once. You're sure to get them mixed up. Do them one at a time.

Wipe dry the area previously covered by the boot of each wire (also wipe inside the boot). Then replace the wire on the distributor cap.

Now dry the wire connection on the top of the coil. It doesn't matter what the coil is, precisely. All you need to know is that it's a dark metal cylinder that can be found at the opposite end of the center wire running out the top of the distributor cap (see sketch).

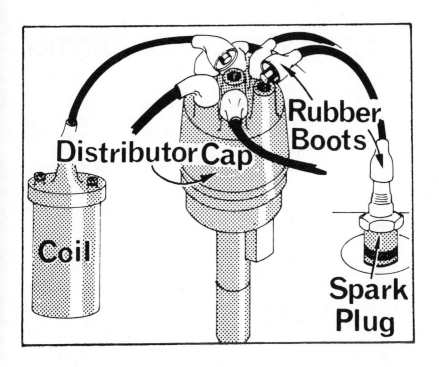

The same drying procedure can be followed around the end of each spark plug. To find the spark plugs, go back to the distributor cap again.

Each of the six or eight smaller wires around the perimeter of the cap connects at the opposite end to one spark plug. Remove, wipe and replace each spark plug wire individually. Do not take them all off at once.

Spark plugs are usually reachable on older models and on four and six-cylinder engines. But on some newer eight-cylinder engines, the spark plugs must be approached from underneath the car. In this case, forget them. Wiping just the center wire of the distributor cap and the opposite end of it at the coil will often do the trick.

6/ Prepare your car for summer

Preparing your car for summer driving is just as important as readying it for winter.

Water-cooled engines, as the term implies, have water running around the engine block and up front through the radiator (see sketch). Air circulating through the honeycomb structure of the radiator dissipates the heat the water has picked up in the engine. The fan (see sketch) helps pull that cooling air through the radiator.

If the belt which drives the fan (and the water pump) is loose or ready to break, you should have it adjusted or replaced. Belts are usually readily visible when you raise the hood. If your car has options like power steering and air conditioning you will see two or three different belts.

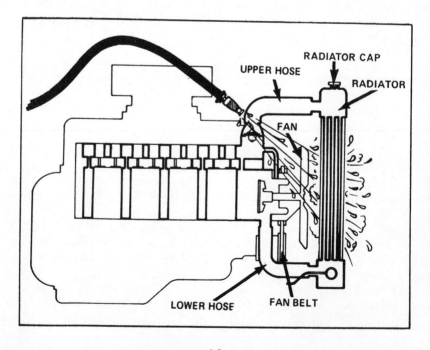

Don't worry about which is which. They should ALL be kept in good shape. If the surface of the belt is peeling or covered with little cracks it should be replaced.

Press down on the belt in the middle of its span. It should "give" about half an inch. If it's too tight or too loose, have it adjusted or replaced. A loose belt can sometimes be heard—either a flopping fluttering sound, a continuous tweet or a high squeal.

Needless to say, you should not try any of these tests (except for sounds) while the motor is running.

Check hoses running from the radiator (see sketch) for cracks, swelling around connecting points and leaks or seepage at those same points.

Bugs and dirt caught on the front of the radiator inhibit the flow of air through it and hamper the cooling system. Clean the radiator occasionally with a high-pressure stream of water from the garden hose. Shoot the water from the engine side of the radiator through toward the grillwork of the car (see sketch).

Check the water level in the radiator; but NEVER remove the radiator cap while the motor is still hot from driving. The coolant inside is under pressure and carelessness may send a jet of boiling water onto your face or hands.

Even after the engine has cooled, the radiator cap should be removed in two steps. Give it just a quarter turn at first. A little safety catch inside should keep it from flying off as the pressure hisses down to a normal level. The cap can then be turned further and removed.

The coolant level should come within about an inch of the bottom ring in the neck where the cap was. If only a quart of coolant is needed, you can add plain water. But if a large amount is needed, or if you are having the radiator system drained (at least once a year), antifreeze should always be added with the water to prevent rust in the system.

In replacing the radiator cap, press down firmly while turning to make a good seal. If the cap is solidly back in place, don't get agitated if the radiator overflows the first couple of times you drive after filling the radiator. It is just seeking its own best level.

If it overflows frequently, have a service station check the cap to see if it is maintaining radiator pressure.

Air-cooled engines do not have radiators or fans. They do, however, have belts which should be checked. And it's smart to see whether mud has been thrown and caked onto the bottom of the engine. If so, it will make the engine run hot and should be either hosed off or chipped away with a screwdriver.

Check the tread on your tires by sticking a pencil lead or something else thin into one of the tread grooves. If it measures 1/16 inch or less, you need new tires.

Find out from your owner's manual or tire warranty how much pressure your type of tire requires for the average load your car carries. (This will change, of course, if you add a load of luggage or a trailer for summer vacation.) Make sure your tires are filled to the correct pressure. Running too hard or too soft can cause tire failure.

Next time you have a few minutes at a service station or garage, have them check fluid levels for the car's rear axle, battery, transmission, power steering and master brake cylinder.

Also have them show you the fluid container for the windshield washer. It is easy to fill, once you know where to find it, and you can carry a little jug of water in the car for emergency refill.

Air conditioners strain a car's cooling system in stop-and-go traffic. To avoid overheating the engine, turn the air conditioning off temporarily or else put the car in neutral during long stops and depress the gas pedal just slightly. This lets you sit still but speeds up the fan, which is pulling air into your cooling system.

Sometimes after becoming quite hot from long driving, an engine will refuse to start up again after a brief stop at a grocery store or restaurant. This is usually because engine temperature has become so high that the fuel is actually percolating. Result is that the engine is flooded.

First raise the hood—it doesn't matter how hot and sunny the day is. The hottest day in recorded history could not approach the temperature under the hood.

Allow a few minutes for the engine to cool. Then follow procedures for a flooded engine. Press the gas pedal all the way to the floor and hold it there while turning the ignition. (This just gives your engine an initial squirt of fuel, not a continuous flow, and allows needed air into the carburetor.)

Before any long trip, have the oil, oil filter and air filter checked. And if the length of the trip will put your car at a mileage total that calls for a tune-up, have the tune-up BEFORE the trip rather than after.

7/ Replace auto headlights

Some do-it-yourself enthusiasts change their own car headlights as a matter of routine. Most of us less ambitious sorts, however, have a service station or garage do it.

But the job is not particularly complicated. And knowing how to change a headlight could come in handy in case of an emergency.

The first things you will need are one or two spare headlights to carry in the car trunk. You can get them at a service station or dealership for anywhere from $1.50 to $4. There are two kinds of headlights. One is only a high or bright beam. The other is a double-filament light that serves as the low-beam lamp until you switch it to high beam with the foot button inside the car.

If your car has double headlights, you'll need one of each kind of lamp. The two lights nearest the center of the car (inboard) are high beam only; the two lights nearest the side of the car (outboard) are combination high-low beam. If the car just has single headlights, you need one of the high-low lights. Make sure you get the right size for your particular car.

The other pieces of equipment you will want to carry include a No. 2 Phillips screwdriver (or in some cases the same size flat-blade screwdriver), a can of penetrating or rust dissolving oil (to help loosen screws) and possibly a small wrench or pliers.

The headlight assembly described here in detail is that used in late model General Motors cars. The systems used by Ford and Chrysler are similar.

The first thing you need to do is turn the lights and the motor off. Then remove the bezel. This is just a funny name for the shiny chrome (or painted) frame around the headlight. The fancier the car, the more difficult the bezel is to remove. It may even be combined with a chunk of grillwork. But look for three to four screws on the bezel itself near the edge of the headlight or in that immediate area.

If the screws are several inches away from the headlight, open the car hood and check to see if the screws are supplemented by a nut-and-bolt arrangement on the back side of the grill. This is where the

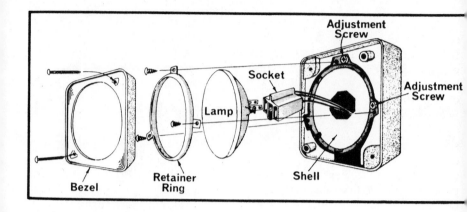

Adjustment Screw

Socket

Adjustment Screw

Lamp

Bezel

Retainer Ring

Shell

wrench or pliers would be needed. Leave the hood up; you may need it open later anyway.

With the bezel removed, look straight on at the front of the headlight. You will see that it is further held in place by a metal collar or retaining ring around the edge of the light itself.

Around the edge of the retaining ring will be several screws.

Two of the screws on the edge of the retaining ring will have a broader head than the others. These are the adjustment screws or pins and are used to aim the headlight. Don't fool with these adjustment screws. You want them to stay just where they are.

The other screws around the edge of the retaining ring (usually three of them) are smaller. These are the ones you take out to release the headlight. They are sometimes wedged in by corrosion or being tightened too far. If you can't turn them, put a couple drops of penetrating oil on each one, give each one a rap with the screwdriver handle to vibrate the oil behind them as well as possible and then try again after a few minutes.

(On some models, the retaining ring may be held additionally at one side by a spring. If so, it will be apparent when undoing the screws does not release the ring. Slip the edge of the ring out from behind the hook of the spring; or just let it hang there by the spring, if you wish.)

After removing the retaining ring, pull the headlight itself out toward you slowly. You will see that it is attached at the back to an electrical cord. The back side of the light is formed into something like the plug at the end of a lamp cord. The end of the cord coming from behind the grill is formed into a socket.

Pull the headlight out of its socket. This is often easier said than done. Use a screwdriver to gently pry the two apart if you have to. Depending on the length of the cord, you may have to work from the back side of the grill.

To install the new headlight, simply reverse the above procedure. Hook the new light to the electrical socket. Let the newly plugged light dangle against the bumper for a minute while you run around and turn the lights on to test the new lamp. (If it doesn't go on, you may have a defective new light or a wiring problem in the car.)

Nestle the new light snugly into the back shell of the retaining assembly, which should still be in position in the car body. (There are little bumps on the back of the new headlight that fit into small depressions in the back shell. Rotate the headlight back and forth until it is seated well.) Then replace the retaining ring with its screws.

If you are working on a Chrysler product, changing a headlight will be slightly different. The smaller screws on the retaining ring are not supposed to be taken entirely out. Just loosen them. Then turn the front portion of the retaining ring about half an inch and pull out. The ring fits onto its screws with hole-and-slot arrangements.

Ford headlight assemblies are similar to those made by General Motors.

If you aren't sure you have installed the new headlight correctly, have a service station check the job as soon as possible. New headlights should also be checked for aim, even though you have not fooled with the adjustment screws. If the aim is not proper, you can blind oncoming drivers.

8/ Jump-start your car

There's no question that winter is hard on a car battery. It takes a good deal of power to crank up a cold, stiff engine.

You can and should learn how to jump start your car—in case service stations are closed or busy. Jump starting is done when your battery is low or dead. It is nothing but starting your car off the power of someone else's battery.

You will need three things: a set of jumper cables (available in any auto supply or department store), an acquaintance who will let you hook up to his battery, and a couple of cloth rags.

A sick battery may be indicated whether the car is groaning as it tries to start or is simply making a click or rat-tat-tat noise. To double check, turn your headlights on and ask a friend to stand in front of the car and watch as you try again to start it.

If there is a battery problem, the lights will dim as you try to start. Any clicking or groaning will also be less audible.

Turn the ignition off and raise the car hood. The battery is a rectangular box located at the front and to one side of the engine. It has two cables running off the top of it and a row of little caps across the top. (Some batteries have caps showing; some have a plastic bar cover over the caps.)

Unscrew the battery caps (usually six of them) or pull off the plastic covers and you should see fluid inside the battery right up to the bottom of the six openings. If you can't see, don't use a match or cigarette lighter for help. A battery gives off an explosive gas that can be touched off by even a cigarette. Use a flashlight instead.

Also use a cloth rag in handling the battery and caps. The contents and any film across the top of the battery are acid and will ruin clothes, gloves and discolor skin.

If you can see no fluid in the battery, fill each of the six openings with clear (better yet, distilled) water. This will help the battery recharge itself after the car starts running again.

Replace the battery caps and

take a look at the posts (usually located at either end of the row of caps) that the battery cables are fastened to (see sketch). Using the cloth rag, grasp the clamps that fit around each post and try to turn them. If they turn easily, they are too loose and need to be tightened. There is a nut and bolt on each clamp for just this purpose. You'll need to dig up a pair of pliers and a wrench.

Now to the actual jump start.

Never jump your car from someone else's battery without asking permission. Ask your friend to bring his car either nose to nose or side to side with your car. Make sure the cars do not touch each other and that both ignitions are then turned off.

Cover the caps of each battery loosely with cloth rags. This cuts down on any explosive fumes circulating around the battery. Some experts say to leave the battery caps in place. Some say to remove

the caps and cover the openings with a rag. A veteran garage man, however, says the safest thing is to combine the two methods by leaving the caps on and covering them with a cloth.

Connect the jumper cables. These are 12 to 15 feet long, one red and one black, ending in heavy spring clamps that look like toothy pliers.

One post of every battery is positive; the other negative. The positive post is slightly fatter than the other one and is marked with a plus sign or the letters "POS." The negative post is usually marked with a minus sign or the letters "NEG."

Connect the red (positive) jumper cable to the positive post of your battery and the positive post of the other battery (install the clamps right over the clamps of the regular battery cable, as shown in sketch). Connect the black (negative) jumper cable to the negative

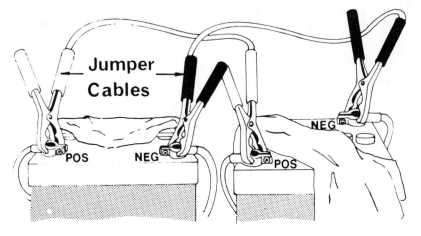

posts of your battery and the other battery.

Positive to positive. Negative to negative.

Have your neighbor start his car after the jumper cables are in place and leave it running while you try to start yours.

After your car is running, remove the negative jumper from your battery and then from the other car's battery. Once that cable is disconnected at both ends, remove the positive cable—first from your car, then from the other.

Do not—repeat, do not—remove both the positive and negative clamps from just one battery, leaving them connected to the other battery. That gives you two "live wires" in your hands and you could easily get a nasty shock.

Now drive to the nearest available place that can check your battery and electrical system to make sure they are operating correctly.

9/ Thaw out that frozen car lock

There are days when you'd much rather not go in to work. But the day the locks on your car doors freeze is always the day you have to be on time.

Some people still make the mistake of pouring a kettle of boiling water down the side of the car window and the door handle. This is bad for two reasons. For some reason, boiling water freezes again quite rapidly. And you can easily crack the window glass by putting it through such extremes of temperature.

The ice inside a lock is usually not thick. The best and fastest method for melting it is to heat your key with a cigarette lighter, then insert the key into the lock. (Wear gloves to keep from blistering your fingers.) It may not work

24

at first, but repeat the process two or three times and the lock should turn.

Once you get the key into the lock, you can even leave it there and heat the exposed end of it briefly while it is in place. That way, it doesn't cool down between lighter and keyhole.

If you don't have a lighter or matches, another method is to put rubbing alcohol on the key or squirt a little shot of it into the keyhole. But don't put fire near the lock afterward.

There are products on the market, too, for unsticking and preventing frozen locks. Some are sprays and some are in squirt cans. They are available at lockshops and department stores and sometimes come in handy for another problem with cold car doors. After you unfreeze the lock and depress the latch button, the door often won't close again because the latch mechanism is frozen or stiff with cold.

Try spraying some of this thawing chemical on the moving parts of the latch on the face of the door edge. Also spray it as far into the door as you can through any crevices around the latch mechanism (see sketch).

The only other alternative is closing the door as far as possible and running the car heater long enough to warm the whole door. Or, if the car is parked close enough to the house, put an extension cord on your hair dryer and haul it out to the car to blow on the door and latch for a while.

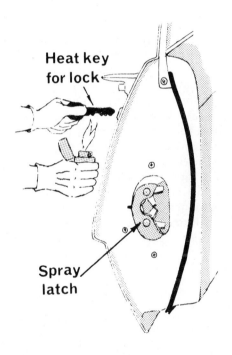

Heat key for lock

Spray latch

10/ Change your car's license plates

The people who thought up using metal nuts and bolts for fastening license plates to cars were all graduates of the Marquis de Sade School of Human Relations.

They were the same people who dreamed up mid-winter deadlines in some states for license plate changeovers.

There isn't much to be done about the deadlines, but fasteners have improved over the years.

Most passenger cars built within the past eight years have a small square plastic nut or "sleeve" that snaps into a square hole in the bumper or plate bracket (see Sketch A).

A slot-headed metal screw screws into the plastic nut, which is supposed to remain in place permanently.

There are two beauties to the plastic nut. First of all, it doesn't rust like the old kind used to do. Second, it stays put as you turn the screw. This means you don't need to reach around behind the

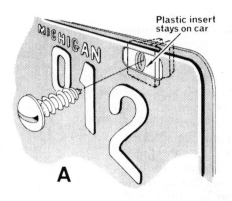

Plastic insert stays on car

A

license plate for any reason.

You approach the whole business straight from the front with a screwdriver. If broken or lost, plastic nuts can be bought for a few cents at auto dealerships.

If you have an older car, you may have one of two other systems. One is a metal bolt and free-spinning nut (see Sketch B). The other is a metal bolt and U-nut (see Sketch C).

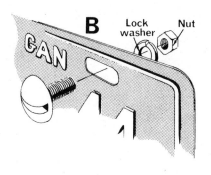

A U-nut will not turn as you turn the screw. But a free-spinning nut will—which means you must reach behind the bumper or plate holder and wrestle the nut with an adjustable wrench or pliers. (To loosen, turn the bolt or screw counter-clockwise as you face the license plate. Hold the nut stationary or turn it clockwise.)

A rusted nut and bolt is almost impossible to remove whole. You can try putting a rust dissolver like penetrating oil (from hardware stores) on it. But you have to apply it where the nut joins the bolt; and this sometimes means crawling under the car to see what you are doing.

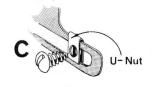

The alternative is a service station or garage, where they will cut the bolt loose.

Unfortunately, you usually cannot replace the old nut and bolt system with one of the newer plastic sleeves because the plastic gismo requires a specially shaped hole. You can, however, go to a brass nut and bolt, which will not rust.

There is no way to tell what system you have just by looking at the license plate, since both old and new methods use a metal, slot-headed screw. The easiest approach is to just try turning the screw with a screwdriver. If it comes right out, fine. If it doesn't, start looking for a rusted U-nut or a free-spinning nut behind the bumper.

11/ Clean aluminum siding

Aluminum siding may require less care than many exterior home surfaces. But it does need some upkeep—especially in industrial areas where corrosive pollution globs onto everything.

Siding should be washed with mild detergent, water and a soft brush about twice a year in normal areas. In industrial areas, change that schedule to four or five times a year.

But suppose you move into a house where the aluminum siding has been neglected for several years and is really caked with dirt and oil. Advice gleaned from four companies dealing in siding is as follows:

All aluminum siding has a paint covering that is baked on at the factory. But different brands use different kinds of paint. And the paint thickness is not always the same either. So whereas one brand may stand up under pretty harsh cleaning, another may not. The answer is to spot test and experiment a bit before tackling the whole house exterior.

Start with mild detergent and warm water used with a soft brush. (Those long-handled brushes that attach to hoses for washing the car are good for doing siding.)

If the mild detergent doesn't work, go to a stronger detergent. A liquid cleaner normally used on floors, in a strong concentration with warm water, will usually do the trick.

If that doesn't work, about the

only alternative is powdered bathroom cleanser used with a soft rag. But this, if used time after time, will take the finish off even the best siding. Using an abrasive compound like cleanser should be a last resort. Don't scrub too long in one spot. And keep in mind that you may have to paint the siding if the cleanser ruins the finish.

Whatever you use to clean, wash from the bottom of the house up. And try to pick a cloudy day for the work.

Working from the bottom up helps prevent streaks. Sure, you will get dirty water dripping down over the areas you have just cleaned. But that is better than soapy water making tracks down through the dirt on lower panels if you start at the top. Clean streaks are harder to get rid of than dirty streaks. A cloudy day simply keeps the streaks from drying so fast.

It is essential to rinse the finished cleaning job well with a hose. Swipe along with the brush, too, to remove all traces of soap. Otherwise, you will have a mess the next time it rains.

If aluminum siding has corroded so badly that dirt has embedded itself in the surface, you probably won't ever be able to get it clean. The only option then will be to paint the siding, if you want a shining clean surface again.

Most companies recommend exterior latex paint for painting over aluminum siding. There shouldn't be any special preparation needed except thorough cleaning, rinsing and drying before the paint goes on.

If siding is extremely corroded, the worst spots are generally up under the eaves of the roof, where rain has not washed the surface. A light sanding with fine-grained sandpaper in those areas may be needed.

Once you do paint aluminum, the surface will eventually require repainting, just as any painted surface does. It should, however, last a bit longer than a paint job on wood, since the expansion and contraction of wood is not a factor.

12/ Install mesh cover to keep leaves out of window wells

Here's a handly little idea for keeping leaves and twigs out of basement window wells.

A mesh cover spanning the recessed area of the window well can save you an unpleasant cleaning chore later.

A variety of materials can be used—screen wire, a wider meshed wire or plastic coated mesh available at hardware and building supply stores.

With a frame house, you can tack or staple the mesh to the bottom edge of the wooden siding; then secure the far edge of the mesh at the outside rim of the window well using bricks, little stakes or whatever is handy and seems safe. See sketch.

With a brick house, you may be able to tack the top edge of the mesh to the top of a wooden window sash.

A brick wall and metal window sash may necessitate building a lightweight wooden frame to fit over the space and hold the mesh

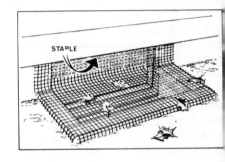

in place.

Prefabricated plastic or fiberglass "dome" covers are supposedly available for basement window wells. But they are a bit difficult to find.

Other possibilities include building a rigid wooden cover which could be removed in summer, or constructing a miniature greenhouse by covering the window well with wood-framed panels of clear plastic or glass. But avoid using glass if the neighborhood is full of children. Rigid covers are always a temptation for children to stand on.

13/ Caulk your home

Caulking and weatherstripping will help seal your home against drafts. Since caulking cannot be applied when the outdoor temperature is below about 40 degrees, it's best to do it on a mild day.

Caulking is the putty-like substance used to cover the little cracks between the body of the house and the window sash (or the door frame). It is usually applied when a house is built, but it should be scraped away and reapplied after a few years have dried and cracked it.

Caulking can be bought in bulk. But do-it-yourselfers usually prefer either cartridges or giant toothpaste tube containers. The squeeze tubes are for small jobs and generally roll up at the end with a key.

Cartridges require a caulking gun, sold separately at hardware stores. (Don't try to use a cartridge without a gun. The plunger inside the cartridge is too hard to push by hand.)

The plunger on the caulking gun is a central rod with teeth or ratchets on one side of it. Turn the rod ratchet-side-up and pull it back as far as it will go (see sketch). Insert the cartridge; then turn the rod so the ratchets face downward (other-

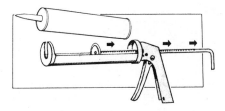

wise the trigger won't engage them to push the plunger forward).

Snip the nozzle of the cartridge at a 45-degree angle; there are little marks on the end to show you where. Also stick an ice pick down the nozzle to break the inner seal where the nozzle joins the cartridge. Then pump the trigger to force out the caulking.

Apply the compound in a continuous "worm" over the crack to be covered. After allowing the caulking to dry a couple of days, a coat of paint over the compound will help keep it flexible. Caulking compound will stick to metal,

31

wood and masonry, but only if the surfaces are dry and fairly clean.

Plain old architectural grade caulking costs 50 or 60 cents a cartridge. Latex and butyl rubber compounds are both more expensive—about $1.40—but are reputed to stay flexible longer.

Weatherstripping comes in many different designs. Some must be nailed into place. But the easiest to handle are flexible, adhesive-backed strips of felt, vinyl or foam rubber.

There are no strict rules about where weatherstripping is to be applied. The idea is simply to stop the drafts.

Stick-on foam strips, for example, can be applied to the windowsill, snug up against the face of the closed window sash. If you don't like the way the stripping looks inside the house, put it on the outside of the window or even inside the groove where the window sash fits—if that won't make it too hard to open and close the window.

If there are directions with the weatherstripping you buy, follow them. If not, ask the salesman at the hardware store.

14/ Remove household uglies - cracked paint, mildew and grease

Painting problems. They seem endless. You wouldn't think a simple wall could play so many dirty tricks.

Recurring spots, mildew, previous coatings can all cause headaches—not to mention backaches. So here are a few hints from a long-time professional in the field:

Spots—Blotches in a new paint job seem to be a particular problem in kitchens, where grease collects on the walls. Often the appearance or reappearance of a spot is followed later by pinpoint bubbles in the paint surface.

One possible cause of this could be a water leak from a nearby pipe or from a bathroom above. If this is the case, nothing short of having the water leak repaired will remedy the situation.

But let's suppose the mark is just a grease spot. Going over a wall with heavy duty detergent before painting doesn't always get it as clean as you might think. Kitchen grease is stubborn and sometimes requires paint thinner or turpentine as a remover.

Once the best possible cleaning job is done, however, one more precaution will keep any remaining grease from spotting your new paint job. That is application of an alcohol based primer-sealer to the wall. This primer-sealer is sometimes called stain kill; and that's exactly what it does. A thin coat of the same thing you plan to use as a finish coat will not do the same job.

Follow the primer-sealer with a coat of enamel undercoat (which is not the same thing as enamel or flat paint), then use the gloss or semigloss enamel that you want. (A "flat" or dull paint is not satisfactory in kitchens because it absorbs grease too readily.)

If you have already painted the whole room and just want to patch an area that keeps spotting, sand the area down and follow the above procedure in the limited space.

Mildew—You will think mildew is just a bit of dirt caught in the paint job until it starts spreading and looking worse with time. Mildew starts in a moist area, but once it takes hold it is quite stubborn and will persist after the moisture problem has disappeared.

Mildew is most commonly found where several layers of wallpaper have been painted over. It takes hold in the glue behind one of the layers of paper and works its way out from there.

The best procedure, although messy, is to remove all the layers of old wallpaper. Then wash the wall with a strong chlorine bleach and water solution to kill the mildew. Follow this with the alcohol based primer-sealer coat mentioned before and then apply the paint you want.

If there is no paper behind your new paint—just plaster—sand the affected area thoroughly, wash with chlorine bleach and water and do the primer-sealer and paint bit. This assumes that there is no chronic problem of a water leak behind that wall.

Previous coats—You can put oil paint over an old coat of latex paint. You can also put latex paint over an old coat of oil paint. Where most people run into trouble is trying to paint over a glossy surface like enamel or varnish or shellac without any special preparation. This is usually not satisfactory, regardless of whether the paint is oil or latex.

The gloss of the old coat of paint must be cut before a new coat will "take". The best method is to sand the old coat—a time-consuming but reliable way. You can also buy paint-on gloss cutters. But if you want to do things the way the professionals do, you will sand.

If you are putting a coat of enamel over a regular, flat finish paint, use a sealer-primer first. Otherwise, you may get an uneven surface where some of the enamel oil has been soaked up by the flat paint beneath.

15/ Fix leaded windows painlessly

Leaded windows are undeniably charming. But they are too expensive to repair, some home owners say.

The objection is valid, since many shops charge $15 an hour to repair such relics.

You must first determine whether the panes in your window are bounded by lead or by zinc.

Scratch the metal hard with your thumbnail. If the metal feels fairly smooth and you can see clear scars or scratches on it afterward, it is lead. Zinc will feel slightly rough and will not yield easily to pressure.

Pull the pieces of the broken pane entirely free of the leading. Wear work gloves; use pliers if you need to.

You should now be able to see the sunken channel in the leading where the glass used to rest. Clear any old putty or cement out of the channel with a screwdriver. Don't press any harder than you must, or you'll take some lead too.

Take the window off its hinges if possible, placing some kind of

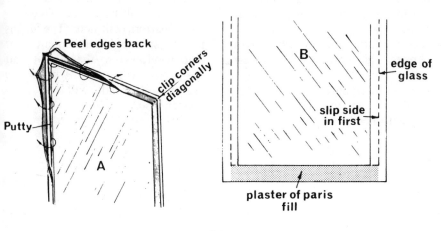

Peel edges back

clip corners diagonally

Putty

A

B

edge of glass

slip side in first

plaster of paris fill

support under the glass section for the remainder of the work.

If the window is true lead, clip the four corners as shown in Sketch A with a pair of wirecutters or a linoleum knife.

Bend the four lead sides upward with your fingers or a pair of pliers. Take it easy. Old leading will sometimes crack if bent too far.

Now measure precisely to determine how large a piece of glass will fit into the opening you have created. Any glass shop will cut a piece to order for you.

Lay the new glass into the cavity. Then pack the channel area beneath the turned-up leading with putty or glazing compound as in Sketch A.

Press the bent leading back down into place with a wooden spoon handle. Do this carefully or you will bend the entire leading network or break the pane you just installed.

This process will squeeze some of the putty out onto the glass but it can be scraped or wiped off later.

Solder the cracks where you clipped the corners. If the lead sides cracked during repair, they can also be soldered.

If your window is zinc, forget trying to bend it.

Measure precisely the top-to-bottom length of the hole to be filled, not counting the recessed channels.

Now measure precisely the width of the hole plus the depth of one channel (usually about an extra one-eighth of an inch). This will allow you to slip the glass into the cavity, side first, without disturbing the surrounding metal.

Fill the bottom channel with plaster of Paris mixed thin enough to pour. Let it harden while you go to the glass shop.

After slipping the new glass into the cavity, center it within the side channels (the top edge of the glass will not extend into its channel). See Sketch B.

Now work putty or glazing compound in under the edge of the leading as well as you can with your fingers. Allow the putty to stiffen for a couple of days; then paint the white edges gray.

If you are replacing an odd piece of glass like a leaf or a flower, the measuring will be tricky. Tracing a paper pattern will help. The idea is to adjust the measurement (for zinc windows) so that about half the glass will come within the channels and half will rest on a plaster base.

16/ Patch minor cracks
in concrete

Did the winter leave your side-walk, patio or concrete stairs cracked and crumbly?

If so, it's best to repair the damage while it's minor. Such cracks are caused by moisture freezing and expanding. Today's small cracks will become wider next winter if not repaired.

There are lots of products on the market for patching concrete. The old standby is regular portland-type cement mixed with sand and water (you can buy sacks that already contain the right amount of sand).

Newer patching compounds are more expensive, but usually very convenient to use. Some come in a puttylike consistency in little buckets. Some are latex based and use a special liquid instead of water. Some are epoxy types that have yet another special liquid plus a hardening agent, and so on.

Whatever you choose, preparation of the old concrete for patching is pretty much the same. The trick is to create as clean a surface as possible.

First brush and scrape away all the loose and crumbled concrete

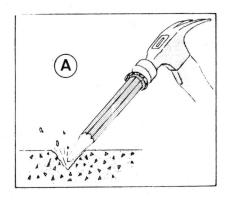

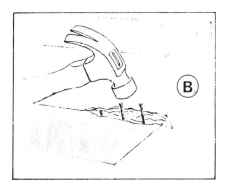

that you can. Then, with a hammer and chisel, form the sides of the crack into a rough "V" (see sketch A). Brush away the new debris you have created. A wire brush is good for this. Get all the dust out too.

37

Most repair manuals say to chisel the crack in a reverse "V" form—wider at the bottom than at the top. But this is almost impossible to do. And worse yet, you run the risk of trapping air bubbles in the crack when you patch it because you can't see exactly what you are doing.

If you are working on a vertical surface like the face of a step, just scrape away all the crumbly material you can. If the seam looks unsound where the vertical portion meets the horizontal surface of the next step, chisel that seam into a small "V." It also helps to drive a couple of masonry nails into the seam as flat up against the vertical surface as possible (see sketch B).

This helps give the patch something to cling to.

If you are using some of the newer concrete patching compounds, follow the directions for use on the package and stick to the mixing proportions they recommend.

If you are using a regular portland cement and sand mixture, follow these recommendations:

Blend the concrete and water to a fairly stiff mixture. It should hold together in your hand in a sort of loose ball if you squeeze it. The more water you mix with concrete, the more it shrinks as it dries; and that's something you don't want.

Next, dampen the surface you'll be patching. Don't make a big puddle; but get the area thoroughly damp. This keeps the old concrete from stealing moisture from the new patching material and gives a better bond.

Plop the patching material into the "V" with a trowel or something similar. Use a generous amount. Poke it and wiggle it around a lot to work it down well into the crack and remove all air bubbles.

Level off the surface of the patch with the edge of the trowel or a board. If working on a vertical surface, create the shape you want with the edge of the trowel. A fairly stiff patching mixture should hold its shape without any wooden forms or bracing material.

Check the patch periodically until it has begun to harden. Then place a piece of cloth or burlap over it and dampen the cloth with a fine spray from the garden hose.

Keep the cloth damp for several days until the concrete patch is completely set or "cured." This is important to keep a portland patch from drying too quickly and developing cracks of its own.

17/ Repaint without "alligatoring"

People who do their own interior painting seem to run into an amazing number of problems.

One of them is referred to by professionals as "alligatoring." This term describes a phenomenon often encountered in older homes where there are several layers of paint—a situation where hairline cracks are present in the old paint surface. A new paint job seems to remedy the problem, until the new paint dries and there are the same old crack lines in the wall. (The word "alligatoring" depicts pretty well what the surface looks like— lines and cross lines in an uneven pattern.)

Alligatoring usually occurs when

a second coat of paint is applied before the first coat is entirely dry. The top surface dries. Then, as the bottom layer of paint dries, it pulls the top surface apart slightly, giving the cracked effect.

(A first coat can feel dry to the touch without really being dry. If

39

you can scratch or peel it by scraping your thumbnail up the wall, the paint is not yet dry.)

Once it happens, alligatoring plagues the housekeeper from then on, unless it is remedied. This is because any new paint—even if applied years later—will sink into the tiny cracks and simply perpetuate the flaws.

The solution is to fill the hairline cracks and build an entirely new surface on which to paint. It is an exasperating and time-consuming process. But it is the only option if those skinny, leafless trees and other odd shapes on your wall are driving you crazy.

First, the old paint must be sanded lightly to make a good gripping surface. You don't need to sand right down to the bare wall. Just roughen the surface slightly with medium-grade sandpaper. Then clean the wall of all the residue from sanding. Use the vacuum cleaner first; follow with a damp rag if necessary.

The next step is to apply spackling compound to the affected area or to the entire wall, depending on how severe the problem is. Spackling compound is a plaster-like substance that can be bought in either powdered form (which must be mixed with water) or in premixed form. The premixed containers are the easiest for do-it-yourselfers.

The spackling compound should be spread over the wall with a very flexible, broad putty knife. Too stiff a spreader will drag the spack-

ling compound out of the cracks you are trying to fill. The blade on the kind of putty knife you want can be bent easily to almost a 90-degree angle. It is more expensive than a cheapo putty knife, but worth it for all the trouble you're going to.

In spreading the spackling compound, use light to moderate pressure on the putty knife. Just enough to give it a slight bend (see sketch). The compound should then fill all the hairline cracks satisfactorily.

Allow the compound to dry at least the amount of time specified on the package. (In fact, ALWAYS read and follow directions on products used in a painting job.) Then sand the dried surface lightly to remove overlap marks and so on.

Believe it or not you're still not ready to paint. The dried spackling compound is very absorbent. It really needs a coat of primer-sealer before painting if you want a nice even, professional-looking job.

The primer-sealer spoken of is not simply a thin coat of whatever paint you plan on using. It is a special preparation. Ask your paint store for a pigmented, alcohol-based primer and sealer (also called a stain kill). It will accept either oil-based or latex paint as a finish coat.

There is one trick to working with an alcohol primer-sealer. It dries very fast—often within 45 minutes to an hour. So you need to cover your surface as fast as possible.

You can use a roller. But the cleanup after using this primer requires denatured alcohol (available at the paint store) and the roller will never really come clean.

You can clean a brush with denatured alcohol. But if you decide on a brush, get a wide one that is natural bristle. Synthetic brushes don't work as well with alcohol primer-sealer.

Let the primer dry completely (check product directions).

Now, chief, you are ready to paint.

18/ Fix stuck fireplace screen

Warm weather is a good time to do some repairs on that pesky fireplace screen that won't slide anymore,

Some screens are free-standing, some are built-in, some mesh panels are pulled to the center by hand, some operate with a pull chain like draperies. Glass screens are something else again and won't be treated here.

The screens that seem the most troublesome are those with pull chains. Nothing serious really. Just annoying.

Chains sometimes get tangled or clogged with carbon and oil deposits. The remedy is to take the whole screen down and give it a good, over-all cleaning.

Fireplace screen styles vary from maker to maker, but the instructions here should apply, with some modification, to most types.

Free-standing screens (those with a complete rectangular frame and little legs in front) are often not attached to the fireplace at all.

Built-in screens are usually flush with the face of the fireplace and

41

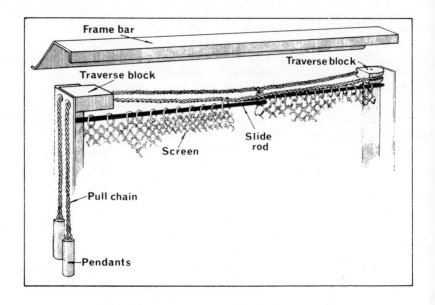

Frame bar

Traverse block

Traverse block

Screen

Slide rod

Pull chain

Pendants

have only a top bar instead of a full frame.

Most built-ins are attached with bolts to the "ceiling" of the fireplace cavity. Get down on the floor and look up behind the screen for a metal brace held to the brick of the fireplace with a bolt—one at each end of the screen. Unscrew the bolt with a wrench or screwdriver and slide the screen and its metal braces forward.

Carry the screen outside and prepare for a messy job. First step is to brush and wipe the entire length of the pull chain with cleaning fluid. Then lubricate it with spray silicone, graphite or light machine oil.

The accompanying sketch shows the pattern that most chains follow—a single length that runs

through two traverse blocks (small braces), one at each end of the frame bar.

Each sliding mesh panel has a small wire circle at its top inside corner. This circle clips through one link in the pull chain (see sketch). The rest of the mesh panel is supported with wire loops over a support bar. Wipe the support bar with cleaning fluid.

You can replace a broken pull chain for about 25 cents a foot. The new chain should be 2½ times the length of the frame.

It's even easier to unclip the pendants at the end of the pull chain and just throw the chain away. Then fasten the pendants to the top inside corners of the mesh panels and operate the panels by hand.

You can rejuvenate mesh panels, unless they are warped and twisted. Put the screen on the ground and clean the panels with a stiff brush and a mild detergent solution.

Rinse with clear water and hang the screen in the sun to dry quick-ly. (If it's a rainy day, blow it with a hair dryer.)

Now spray the mesh with special paint that resists high temperature. Black, copper and brass sprays are on the market (usually at fireplace shops).

HERE'S HOW TO:

19/ Rebuild broken staircase banister

A staircase banister that's losing its vertical spindles looks about as appealing as a person who's losing his teeth.

There are different ways to build a banister. But two methods are probably most common.

The first is with channels and spacer blocks. The vertical spindles in a banister are called balusters. In this construction, the ends of each baluster fit into channels or grooves that run the length of the stair line and the underside length of the handrail.

Between the ends of balusters is a small piece of wood called a spacer block. It is sunk into the channel and held in place with glue or nails. The same arrangement is used in both stair line and handrail channels. The ends of each spacer

block are slanted or beveled to accommodate the slant of the stairway (see sketch A).

When a baluster falls out, it is

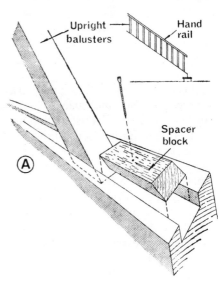

Upright balusters

Hand rail

Spacer block

Ⓐ

usually because a spacer block is loose or has come out entirely. The remedy in this case is simple. Either tack the old spacer block back in place or cut a new one. Pry another block out of the channel to use as a pattern for the replacement. (A thin putty knife or screwdriver will usually work the block loose.)

If all the spacer blocks are in good shape, chances are your whole staircase is starting to sag, widening the gap between stair and handrail. The only permanent solution is to have a professional carpenter or contractor shore up the weak portions of the structure. But, in the meantime, you can try making a temporary repair by removing a spacer block and slipping a thin square of cardboard (a "shim") under the bottom end of the affected baluster.

This may raise the baluster enough in its bottom channels that the top end of the spindle will once more come within the channel of the handrail.

Some banisters do not use slanted channels and spacer blocks. Instead they have balusters that appear to sit flush against the stepping surface of each stair. (The handrail may or may not have spacer blocks in it.)

In this construction, the bottom end of the baluster usually has a small knob or dowel on it that fits into a hole drilled in the stair surface (see sketch B).

It is more difficult to repair one

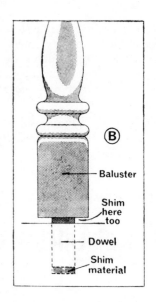

of these balusters. Check for any loose or missing spacer blocks in the handrail. But if the diagnosis is a sinking staircase, you may want to slip a circle of cardboard into the hole in the step.

The problem is that you will create a gap between the "finished" portion of the baluster and the stair step (as shown in sketch B). You may be able to hide this to an extent by cutting thin wooden pieces to fill in the gap. But it will require some very exact measuring, some sanding and painting; and the repair may always look a bit rough.

There is one more thing to check before giving up and calling a carpenter.

Curving handrails are often put together in sections, each section held to the next with some kind of complicated internal gismo. If the connecting rod becomes loose, the balusters can start falling out.

Find the seam in the handrail (it should be readily visible from the top side). Then look on the bottom side of the handrail near the seam for a hole. Inside the hole, you should find a nut (as in nut and bolt).

Turn the nut to tighten the connection. This is easier said than done, since the nut is generally recessed and hard to reach. Try using needle-nosed pliers or a small screwdriver and hammer.

20/ Tighten sagging cane chairs

Cane bottom chairs are both a joy and a grief to those who buy or inherit them. The intricately woven strands of cane look great but are expensive to replace.

When a cane seat starts to sag with use, extra strain is put on the strands around the chair edge. It doesn't take a crystal ball to see a broken seat in the near future.

Bringing the cane up tight and level again will help preserve the chair. It's a simple process of soaking and drying.

Mix as much warm water and plain glycerin as you will need, using a ratio of one ounce glycerin (available at drug stores) to two quarts water.

Soak two towels in the solution

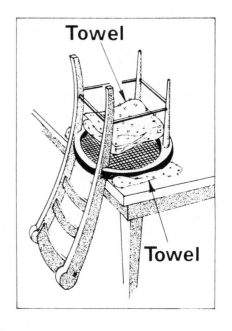

Towel

Towel

45

for each chair being treated. Place one wet towel on the corner or edge of a table; turn the chair over, resting the seat on the towel; put the remaining wet towel on the upturned underside of the chair seat. (See sketch.)

Let the cane absorb the water and glycerin for about half an hour or until the fibers are flexible. Then simply set the chair aside to dry for about 24 hours; the cane shrinks as it dries. An electric fan will speed the process.

Cane that has been varnished will not absorb the water and glycerine. But check the underside of a varnished seat; it may not have been painted. If it appears untreated, try a wet towel against just the one side. It will often still do the job.

21/ Refinish hardware in older homes

Part of the charm of an older house is the hardware in it. But invariably, previous owners or renters have slopped one or more coats of paint over doorknobs, hinges and window fasteners.

Paint thinner won't touch the old paint and scraping is not practical. But you can get it off of most metals with paint and varnish remover—that gloop that you use to take the finish off of old furniture.

Paint remover may cause discoloration of some metals. But metal polish will usually bring the hardware back to its original color. Test a small or hidden spot on the metal to see what the reaction is.

Hinges and some metal fasteners can usually be removed by undoing the screws that hold them in place. Do remove hardware that you can. It makes things much easier.

Drop the hardware right down into the container of paint remover and let it soak for a few minutes. (Most brands of remover have directions that say how long it takes them to work.)

Arm yourself with rubber gloves, an old toothbrush and steel wool. Then retrieve the hardware from the gloop and scrub it well with the steel wool. Some paint removers are flammable, so read directions and heed any warnings.

After all the old paint has been loosened, wipe the hardware as clean as possible with a dry cloth. Then wash it with soap and water. The best paint removers will wash away well. Others leave a wax residue which must be removed with lighter or cleaning fluid.

If you can't take the hardware off of the door or window, you can still use paint remover. But the job is a little trickier, because one slip will take the paint off of the woodwork too.

Protect the wood around the painted metal with wide borders of masking tape. Then carefully brush the paint remover onto the metal, allowing it the recommended time to work.

Wipe the metal clean with steel wool and a dry cloth. Several applications may be necessary.

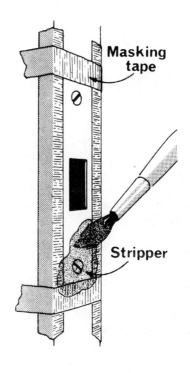

Masking tape

Stripper

22/ Clean oil paintings

The only oil painting you possess may be a too-blue seascape by great-aunt Minnie. But it probably has sentimental if not monetary value. So why not take a few tips on oil painting care from professionals.

Edward R. Gilbert, chief conservator for Greenfield Village and Henry Ford Museum in Dearborn, Michigan, says do-it-yourself cleaning agents should not be used on oil paintings. Dust should be removed from the picture face by brushing the painted surface lightly with a clean, soft camel hair brush (like a large water-color brush.)

A cloth, or even a feather duster, can catch on little flecks of paint and "chip" them off the surface. Using a cloth also requires enough pressure to flex the canvas, causing cracks in the paint.

To help keep oils clean, hang

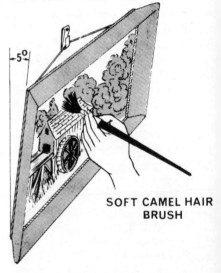

SOFT CAMEL HAIR BRUSH

paintings at a slight angle (about five degrees) so it will be harder for dust to settle on the surface (see sketch).

If a painting is in good condition, the back of it can be cleaned carefully with the vacuum cleaner using reduced pressure.

Dust often settles against the back of a canvas where it meets the stretcher (the wooden support structure to which the painting is tacked). Dust can retain moisture, which causes damage, so it is smart to install a dust cover over the back of a painting.

The cover can be a simple sheet of cardboard fastened to either the back of the frame or the stretcher (whichever is handy). A good material to use is a light foam substance encased in paper and available at some art stores.

Attach the dust cover with screws; nails or staple guns jar an old or delicate painting too much on insertion. Cardboard expands and contracts with moisture, so make the holes in the cardboard a bit larger than needed for the size screw used.

Do not expose oil paints to extreme temperature or humidity changes. Also keep them away from heaters and sunlight.

Never carry a frame by its top edge; support the entire structure. The same thing applies to unframed paintings.

In case of a tear, medical adhesive tape can be applied to the back of the canvas to keep torn fibers in position until the painting can be restored by a professional.

HERE'S HOW TO:

23/Mend joints in creaky chairs

Do your joints creak when you sit down?

You may not be able to reverse the aging process within your own body, but you can reinforce the joints in squeaking wooden chairs.

A loose rung on a chair is best repaired when it can be removed entirely. After removal, scrape the old glue from the rung end and from the hole in the chair leg. Try not to enlarge the hole in the process.

New glue can then be applied liberally to both surfaces. (White vinyl, epoxy or formaldehyde glues would be good choices.) But if the hole is too large for the rung, you can "fatten" the end of the rung in a couple of ways.

One method is to apply glue to the rung end, then wrap the end with a length of sewing thread (you can also use a strip of nylon stocking or a couple threads of steel wool). Allow the glue to dry; then put fresh glue over the threads and inside the hole.

Another way is to install a wedge in the end of the rung, forcing it to expand as it's inserted in the hole (see sketch A). Saw a slot in the end of the rung and insert the cut-off end of a wooden clothespin (skinny end first). Coat the rung and hole with glue as before. When the rung is positioned in the hole, give the outside of the chair leg a good rap to secure the rung and drive the wedge back into the sawed slot.

A rope tourniquet will help hold the joint firm until the glue dries. Tie a rope loosely around the outside of the chair legs, protecting the finish with scraps of cloth or paper. Use a stick or pencil to twist the rope tight across the center, bracing the stick against the rung to keep it from unwinding. (See sketch B.)

If the offending rung cannot be removed for repair, try drilling a hole into the joint through the side of the leg. Drill only as far as the rung end; then inject glue as forcefully as possible into the joint. Special "squirters" are available at some hardware stores; or you might want to try an old ketchup or mustard dispenser. Fill in the hole with wood putty that matches

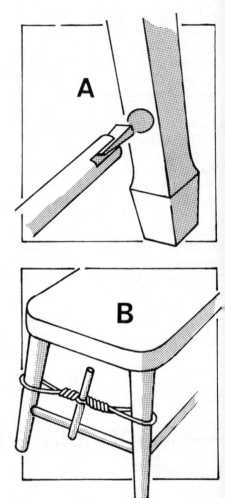

the chair finish as closely as possible.

These procedures also apply to legs that fit a socket in the bottom of the chair seat.

Wobbly joints where legs are attached to the corner of the seat

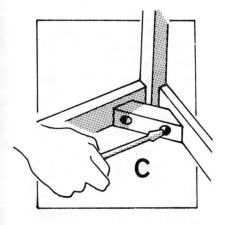

frame can best be fixed with corner braces as shown in sketch C. Secure the braces with both glue and screws. Prepare a path for each screw by drilling a hole slightly smaller in diameter than the width of the screw. Be careful not to drill clear through the side of the chair into the finish.

24/ Replace vacuum cleaner belts

A busy housewife probably uses her vacuum cleaner as much or more than a businessman uses his car.

If you have an upright vacuum with a rotating brush on the bottom, one of the things you should do once a year is replace the belt that makes the brush whirl. Constant use makes the belt stretch and sometimes even break.

Different brands have different types and locations for the belt. But generally the belt looks like a big, thick rubber band and runs from the shaft of the motor to a point on the brush roller. (If your upright vacuum is not doing a good job, turn it on, turn it over and look at the brush roller. Don't stick your fingers in it. The roller should be going around. If not, you probably have a broken belt.)

The belt is usually simple to replace. Yet on some models where a particular twist in the belt is required, people continually put the thing on backward.

When installed backward, the belt makes the brush turn in the wrong direction. So instead of flipping dirt back toward the air intake of the vacuum, the brush scoots dirt away from and ahead of the vacuum.

Consult your owner's manual if you still have it. Otherwise, turn the vacuum over and look for a partial plate covering the bottom of the appliance. Naturally, unplug the vacuum before working on it.

Remove the partial plate. Sometimes it snaps off; sometimes screws must be unfastened. Still others have a couple of small metal arms called cam locks that pivot on a pin and operate much like the lock on a window.

The next step, on most upright models, is to remove the brush roller. It often just yanks straight out. If not, there are probably spring clips on the ends that must be pressed in while you pull.

If the belt is buried down on the side somewhere and looks like it will be hard to reach, take the vacuum to a shop. It won't cost much to have them do the job for you.

But if the belt is easily accessible, there's no reason you can't make the change yourself. Remove the belt from the brush roller and the shaft of the motor. Jot down the make and model of your vacuum and take the note and the old belt to the vacuum shop with you so the belt can be matched for size and style.

When installing the new belt,

look on the bottom of the vacuum (near where the belt runs) for any arrows or directions printed on the vacuum. Follow them to the letter. Some belts turn one way; some the other.

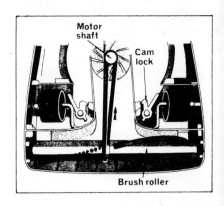

The Hoover upright shown in the sketch is an example of the type of arrangement that requires a twist in the belt, since the belt runs vertically around the brush roller and horizontally around the motor shaft.

Loop the new belt over the brush roller first. Then snap the roller back into place. At this point, the "bottom" leg of the belt will be closer to the body of the vacuum than the "top" leg of it is.

On the model shown in the sketch, the directions say this bottom portion of the belt should approach the motor shaft from the right (there is a little arrow to point the way). Stretch the belt up and loop it over the groove in the motor shaft. The finished job, with this particular upright model, should look like the sketch shown here.

Replace the protective plate. If you can't get the plate back on, or if the plate does not cover the newly installed belt, you may have put the brush roller in backward. With most models, the brush snaps in only one way. But on others it is possible to switch ends of the roll-er. The remedy is simple. Just take the roller out and put it back correctly.

One more thing to check. The bristles of the brush roller should stick out past the line of the protective plate on the bottom of the vacuum. If they don't, they have worn down and you are not getting the cleaning power you should. A shop can replace the brushes for a reasonable price.

25/ Repair loose countertops

The plastic laminate on a countertop occasionally comes loose at the corner. When it does, it's nothing but an increasing annoyance. Sleeves catch on it. Food and water collect under it.

Refastening of the laminate can usually be accomplished with contact cement. Contact cement is the kind where you coat both surfaces to be joined, allow the two glued portions to dry separately, then smack the two surfaces together.

Many contact cements are quite flammable. So heed any warnings printed on the label.

Since countertop laminate cracks if you try to bend it too far, lift the loose corner up only far enough to slip a small paint brush

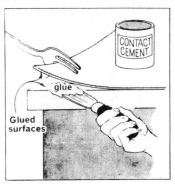

full of cement under it.

Leave a blob of glue under the laminate. Then mash the countertop material down to spread the blob evenly. Lift the laminate up again and prop it with a pencil stub, an old fork or a putty knife to allow the two glue surfaces to dry. Make sure glue is extended clear to the edge of the counter and the laminate.

After the glue has dried for the time recommended on the label, press the laminate firmly back down, working from the center of the counter out toward the edge. A rolling pin can help you get firm, even pressure.

If your countertop problems are more severe—burns, buckling, warping—you may have to give up the idea of doing anything yourself.

Such problems usually mean replacement of an entire section of laminate. It's evidently the very devil to remove, coming off in bits and pieces with great difficulty.

26/ Rid your house of wasps

The planning sessions for D-Day were probably nothing compared to the cumulative hours invested in strategy each summer by Americans Against Those Darned Wasp Nests.

Everyone has his pet method for attacking a wasp nest (which always seems to appear in the least desirable place—in the attic, on the back porch, under the second-story eaves). The most common method, however, is to let somebody else do it.

Here are some hints for the brave.

One "handyman" book suggests hanging strips of flypaper around an indoor nest, changing the flypaper frequently until all resident wasps have been trapped. Then the nest can be knocked down, doused with kerosene or lighter fluid and burned.

For an outside nest, the book says to put a ladder up (if needed) during the day. Then at night, while the wasps are snoozing in the nest and dreaming of the people they'll sting, you put on a hat, veil, gloves and long-sleeved shirt. Un-

der cover of darkness, you climb the ladder, clip the nest free and let it fall into a plastic or heavy paper bag.

The book then says to "immediately douse the nest with kerosene and set it on fire." One assumes, however, that this is best done after descending from the ladder.

E. C. Martin, professor of entomology (bugs) at Michigan State University, says these procedures sound overly complicated to him. His first bit of advice is to pick up a can of wasp spray at the grocery or drug store. NOT an all-purpose bug spray, but one specifically marked for wasps, hornets and bees.

He says there are three common wasps: Hornets, which build big round flakey-looking nests up in trees; yellow jackets, with the yellow and black striped bodies, and Polistes wasps, which are a sort of russet color and are sometimes called red wasps.

A hornet nest has a hole in the bottom of it about an inch in diameter. Wait until night, when the hornets are asleep and spray up into the hole for as long as your nerve lasts. Give the outside of the nest a parting shot with the spray before you run like the devil. The idea is that the hornets will not fly out the hole against the spray.

The same theory applies to yellow jackets, which nest in the ground (often near tree roots) and have about a one-inch opening to the nest. Again, wait until evening and then spray into the hole.

Red wasps are different. Martin says it is best to attack their nests during the day while the adults are out gathering food. If you get to the nest in early summer while it is small, the population of the nest may be only two or three adults. The longer you wait, the more wasps develop.

Once you have knocked down the nest, spray the area if possible to prevent a return engagement. Then keep an eye peeled for the returning adults and knock them off one by one with the spray. Also install screen wire over all attic vents.

As for burning the nests, this is fine. But Martin says he just stomps on them.

27/ Fix a "singing toilet"

There are few things more annoying than a "singing" toilet. The sound of water constantly running through a toilet tank is music to no one's ears—especially since it increases the water bill.

Two basic assemblies control the water in a toilet tank--the flushing mechanism and the refill mechanism. We'll talk about half the equipment in this chapter and the other half in the next chapter.

The flushing mechanism may be your culprit. This is certainly the case if you have to jiggle the toilet

handle each time to stop the toilet from running.

First, take the top off the tank and flush the toilet once to watch what happens. If your toilet is of the most common style, you will see a rubber stopper, called a flush ball, rise from the bottom of the tank to let the water out.

Next, look for a small, faucet-type handle on the water pipe leading to the toilet and shut off the water supply coming into the tank. Flush the tank once more to clear it of all water.

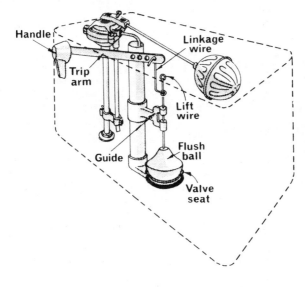

Now begin checking.

Lift the flush ball and examine it to see if it has deteriorated. If the surface has become rough and crumbly, buy a new one; the old one unscrews from the wire stem. It's a good idea to also give the rim of the flush ball seat (the drain hole at the bottom of the tank) a quick scrubbing with steel wool to keep it smooth.

Working back along the system, check the lift and linkage wires to make sure they are not bent. If they are, you can buy new ones at any hardware store for a dollar or less. (Sometimes, if they don't seem to be sliding well, a thin coat of petroleum jelly helps, too.) If you install new wires, make sure the linkage wire gives the flush ball leeway enough to drop back down completely onto the valve seat.

If the flush ball is not dropping back squarely onto the valve seat, check the wire guide—the little metal clip with an eye in it that holds the lift wire straight. Loosen the screw holding the guide in place and move the guide back and forth until the flush ball is dropping the way it should. (Be sure to tighten the guide screw again when you are through.)

Finally, determine whether you need a new handle. (The handle on the outside and the long metal trip arm on the inside are all one unit.) The handle assembly shouldn't rattle back and forth very much. A nut screws onto the back side of the handle, just inside the tank wall. If tightening this nut doesn't help the situation, the handle assembly is inexpensive to replace and one size fits most toilets.

28/ Fix toilet fill unit

If you are treated to the high-pitched serenade of water running through the toilet tank day and night, and you've determined that the problem is not in the flushing mechanism, water may be escaping through the overflow pipe.

The last chapter dealt with the flushing mechanism. This one looks at the refill unit.

Take the top of the tank off and check the water level inside. It should stop about a half inch short of the top of the overflow pipe. If it doesn't, there is probably trouble in the inlet valve which, as its name implies, lets water back into the tank after flushing.

The inlet valve is controlled by that long metal arm with the float at the end of it. As the water level rises, so does the float arm, eventu-

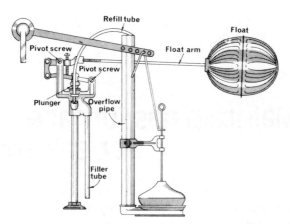

Refill tube · Float · Pivot screw · Float arm · Pivot screw · Plunger · Overflow pipe · Filler tube

ally shutting off the water before it runs over the top of the overflow pipe.

So as a first step, while water is still in the tank, lift up slightly on the float arm. If this stops the "singing," adjustment will be fairly simple.

Locate thefaucet-type handle on the pipes leading into the toilet tank and shut off the water supply. Now flush the toilet to clear the tank of water. Unscrew the float from the end of its arm and shake it. If it has water inside, it is leaking and should be replaced.

If the float is in good shape, try bending the float arm downward from about the middle until the bulb rides a half inch to an inch lower. Then turn the water back on to see if the problem has been remedied.

If not, you may need to replace the washers on the plunger.

The sketch shows a common mechanism style. There are others. But to change the plunger on this system, remove the two pivot screws that hold the linkage end of the float arm onto the valve brace which looks sort of like an uneven tuning fork. The linkage itself runs through the slotted top of the plunger. Remove the float arm and its linkage, sliding it out of the plunger top.

Pull the plunger up to remove it. On the bottom of the plunger (or sometimes down in the recess) is a rubber or leather washer (small disk), with another washer at about the halfway point on the plunger. Replace these with the same type washers. To be sure, you might take the old washers to the nearest hardware store and ask the clerk to match them.

When you put the equipment back together, make sure the refill tube (see diagram) is feeding into the overflow pipe. This arrangement keeps a correct water level in the waste pipe trap, preventing sewer gas from escaping into the house.

29/ Maintain gas furnace at peak efficiency

Among the most common heating setups is a gas furnace hooked to a forced air system.

A gas furnace should be checked by either the gas company or a heating contractor at least every other year. Once a year is even better.

Any adjustment of valves controlling the gas and air mixtures in the furnace should be left to an expert. He should also check the safety device that shuts off the gas flow in case the pilot light goes out. (You should, by the way, leave the pilot light on all year to avoid condensation in the furnace.)

But there are a few simple things the home owner can do to keep the system efficient. Chief among these is changing the air filter, a large square of woven fiberglass strands framed in cardboard and usually covered with a metallic mesh. It should be changed two or three times during the heating season. (See sketch A.)

The filter is generally located just inside the cold air return duct, where air enters the furnace to be warmed and, later, sent back into the house. A dirty filter will slow circulation and sometimes make a furnace run twice as long as it should.

To find the filter, look in the blower compartment of the furnace. This is sometimes at the bottom. Just open all the little doors and snap-out grille sections on the furnace until you find it.

The blower area is the one that contains a large, round metal device that looks like an enclosed

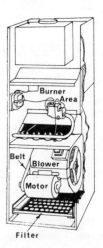

squirrel or gerbil cage. In different models the filter sits at different angles. But it should be in plain view.

The size of the filter should be printed on the cardboard frame. If not, measure the filter by length, width and thickness (the replacement must be the same size).

When installing the new one, check the cardboard frame for a little arrow marked "air flow." Turn the filter so that air flowing into the furnace from the duct will follow the direction of the arrow.

The blower motor should also be oiled once a year, unless it is the sealed type, which has no oil holes.

If it can be oiled, you will see a little hole (about 1/4-inch in diameter on the motor body near each end. These holes are usually covered with a flip-top or snap-off cap and are sometimes marked "oil." Two to three drops of light motor oil a YEAR will suffice.

Now to emergencies. What do you do when the furnace suddenly won't operate?

With gas fuel, which is highly explosive, most remedies should be left to the gas company, which will send a man out to reignite pilot lights (sometimes for free, sometimes for a fee, depending on the company).

But first check to see whether the pilot light is still burning. To find the pilot, follow the gas line to where it enters the furnace, remove the nearest panel and look in the burner section (sketch A) for a skinny, 1/4-inch aluminum tube with a flame at the end of it. The flame should be fairly visible, so if you see no fire in the burner section at all, the pilot is probably out.

If so, and if you can smell gas, it is a good idea to shut off the gas to the furnace.

This can be done with an L-shaped handle located near the furnace on the gas line. (This handle will also help you identify the gas pipe, which is about the same size as a water pipe.) If the handle is turned parallel to the pipe, the gas is on; turning it at a right angle to the pipe shuts the gas off. (See sketch B.)

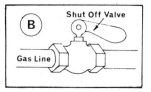

If the pilot light is burning, look for a switch (just like a light switch) on the side of the furnace or located on the wall nearby. It controls electricity to the motor and may have been turned off by a child. (Not all furnaces have such a switch.)

Next, check the circuit breaker or fuse for the furnace. This is usually located with or near the other household fuses, and should be labeled. Flip the circuit breaker to "on" or replace the blown fuse. If it blows again right away, there

Contact
Points
(Slip bill
between)

C

may be a serious problem in your wiring.

Finally, check the thermostat. Remove its cover. If you see a little capsule of liquid, you have a mercury vial control and there is likely no problem with it (nothing you can do about it anyway).

But if the device is a sort of U-shaped prong, turn the dial higher until you see two contact points (about the size of a pin head) come together. If these points are dirty, they may not be functioning. So slip a crisp dollar bill or a business card between the points; hold the points together and slide the bill back and forth to clean the surfaces. (See sketch C.)

If none of these measures works, call a serviceman.

30/ Properly maintain your oil furnace

Basic maintenance steps for an oil furnace and checkpoints in case of unexpected trouble are much the same as for a gas furnace, described in another chapter. But there are a few differences.

As with a gas furnace, changing dirty air filters (if you have a forced air system) is perhaps the simplest and most important maintenance step. This should be done two or three times each heating season.

The blower motor should be oiled sparingly once a year. Look for one or two little quarter-inch holes (sometimes capped) near each end of the motor.

Your equipment should be checked by a serviceman at least once a year.

If an oil furnace stops unexpectedly, take the following steps:

1. Check the oil supply to make sure you're not out of fuel. The oil tank may be located in the basement, garage or sometimes outside the house. A gauge on the tank will show whether it is empty. But to make sure the needle isn't stuck,

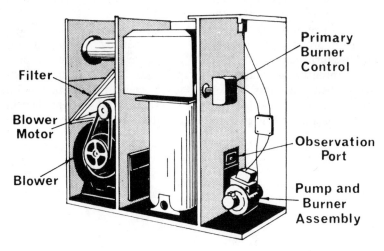

Filter

Blower Motor

Blower

Primary Burner Control

Observation Port

Pump and Burner Assembly

give the gauge a slight tap or give the side of the tank a whack near the gauge.

2. Check the household fuse or circuit breaker box to see whether the fuse controlling electrical portions of the furnace has blown. If so, replace it (or flip the circuit breaker back to "on"). Before replacing the fuse, turn the home thermostat down low; after the new fuse is in place you can turn it back up. If the fuse blows again right away, there may be a wiring problem requiring a serviceman.

3. Look for a switch (looks just like a light switch) on the side of the furnace or on the wall or rafters nearby. This also controls electricity to the furnace and may have been turned off by someone.

4. A box about eight inches square, called the primary burner control or relay, is often located just outside the furnace, sticking out of the smoke stack. On some newer furnaces, it is inside near the pump-burner assembly. There is a button on the primary control box to restart the furnace.

Wait 20 minutes after the furnace stops; then push this button (or move it sideways). The waiting period is important, as this gives oil

fumes in the furnace a chance to clear—a safety factor.

Some repairmen say the button should be pushed only once; others say twice is all right. But no more than twice; and you should wait another 20 minutes before the second attempt.

5. Sometimes there is an overload button or switch on the burner pump motor, which is located on the outside wall of the furnace or, in newer models, just inside (see sketch). This button (often red) should be pressed once.

If, after pushing these various buttons, you are not sure whether the oil is burning, you can look into the firebox through a little spring-trap door—the observation port (see sketch).

But wait five minutes after pushing the button before you open the port. Oil sometimes "puffs" when it catches fire. If you don't give it that five minutes, you may get a face full.

6. Finally, check the household thermostat by running it up five degress over the present room temperature. If the furnace does not react, clean the contact points in the thermostat as described in the chapter on gas furnaces.

31/ Fix a rackety radiator, cold boiler

If you have a steam system, the thing in the basement or utility room that you call a furnace is actually a boiler—a big tank of water with a heating element attached. As the water boils, steam rises up a main pipe, called a header, to warm the radiators, condense back into water and run back down to the boiler. (See sketch A.)

Boilers come in many different shapes and sizes and use different fuels. But they have several things in common.

One is the gauge glass, a clear tube hanging on the side of the boiler (see sketch B). The water level in the gauge glass corresponds to the water level in the boiler. If the boiler has an automatic feed device, the water will stay at about the one-third level on its own.

But if the boiler has a manual feed—and most small to medium homes do—you should keep the water level about half way up the glass. Some boilers may need filling once a day; Others maybe once a week. Check yours once a day until you learn its cycle.

To fill the boiler, find the refill valve (looks just like the handle on an outdoor water hydrant) on the water line leading into the boiler (sketch B). Wait till the heat has been off about 10 minutes. Turn the valve just a bit, until you can hear water running SLOWLY into

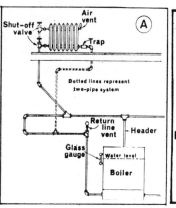

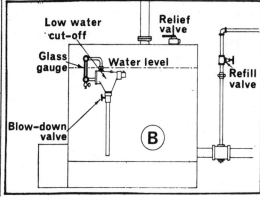

the tank. DO NOT turn the faucet on full blast. This floods the warm or hot tank with a sudden volume of icy water, creating stress that could crack the boiler.

Even worse is adding water to a hot boiler that has run dry. If, when you check, you can see no water at all in the glass, turn the household thermostat way down and wait for the boiler to cool.

If the boiler is standing free, wait till you can put your hands on it without being burned; if it's enclosed in a metal cabinet, wait until the cabinet is no longer warm. Again, add water slowly.

Boilers should not actually run dry. There is a safety device on many of them that is supposed to shut off the heat when the water level gets low (see low water cut-off, sketch B). But sometimes this device becomes fouled and quits working.

To keep this from happening, you should clear the dirty water and sediment from the cut-off mechanism once every two to four weeks by opening the blow-down valve.

This is a faucet-looking handle (sketch B), spring loaded (which means it will close by itself if you let go of it), and may or may not have a long pipe "spout" attached to it. Turn the household thermostat up to test the cut-off while draining it. Make sure the glass gauge is at the halfway mark. Place a bucket under the blow-down valve and let the water out of it

until the water runs clear. The heat should shut off as the water level gets low. Afterward, bring the water level in the glass gauge back up to half.

There is also a way to drain the actual boiler. But unless the water in the glass is the color of chocolate milk, it is best to leave this to the judgment of the serviceman who checks (or should check) your equipment once a year. Reason: Adding fresh water to the boiler also adds all the chemicals that water contains and contributes to "liming" the inside of the boiler.

A good safety check to make: Find out if the relief valve on the boiler is working. This valve is designed to let off excess steam if the boiler builds up too much pressure. It is a round gismo with a small lever on top, sometimes found atop the boiler, sometimes on the side (sketch B). While the heat is on, lift up or push down briefly on the lever. It should hiss. If it doesn't, have the valve replaced or repaired.

Now to the radiators. There are two different kinds—one-pipe and two-pipe. Sketch A shows, basically, a one-pipe system; the dotted lines show where outlets are in a two-pipe system.

With one-pipers, you should keep the shut-off valve (sketch A) either all the way open or all the way closed. Incoming steam and outgoing condensate use the same opening; if it isn't open wide, the steam and water will "fight" each other, causing all kinds of racket.

The radiator air vent (sketch A) lets air flow out as steam flows in. When hot steam hits the air vent, it's supposed to close; so if you see steam coming from the vent, the temperature control inside it is broken and the vent should be replaced (about $3 to $6; take it along for the hardware store to match).

If the air vent is clogged, the radiator will be cold because the steam can't get in. To check the air vent, turn the radiator OFF, let it cool, unscrew the vent and try to blow through it. If you can't, get a new vent.

To help remedy loud pounding in a one-pipe system, check the return line vents (see sketch A) near the boiler. They are somewhat like the radiator vents. Also, prop the legs of the radiator so that it's either exactly level or tips ever so slightly toward the single pipe.

A two-pipe radiator usually has no air vent. Rather, there is a fist-sized trap on the outflow line at the bottom of the radiator (sketch A). This, like a vent, helps control how much steam enters the radiator and has a temperature sensitive device inside.

If it breaks down or fails "open," the affected radiator will heat like crazy while others are relatively cool—because steam is going through and through the radiator with nothing to stop it. One of the return line vents near the boiler will probably also be spouting steam.

If the trap fails "closed," the radiator will fail to heat. A serviceman can replace a trap or you can unscrew the top of it with a wrench and take the top to a dealer for replacement. But turn the radiator off first and let it cool.

Two-pipe radiators should be either level or tipped just slightly toward the lower outflow pipe. The shut-off valve on a two-piper CAN be set halfway open or closed, since condensate leaves by the lower pipe.

32/ Drain your water heater (and increase its efficiency)

There's probably no such thing as Be Kind to Your Water Heater week. But your water heater does need some loving attention to keep on working the way it should.

The only things you need to worry much about are keeping the area around the water heater clean and well-ventilated and draining the water out of the heater every six months or so.

This draining helps remove sediment from the tank. If allowed to build up in the tank, the sediment will reduce the amount of hot water you are getting and will cause other more serious problems.

If you have not drained your water heater in two years, have a serviceman do it. In that long a time, the rubber washers or rings in the drain valve may have become brittle or caked with sediment and you may not be able to get the valve completely shut again if you try it yourself. After having the serviceman out, you can do it yourself once every six months.

This is the procedure:

Up at the top of the water heater are two pipes. One feeds cold water into the tank. The other sends hot water out of it. You can tell one pipe from the other by touch after you let about a gallon of hot water run out of a faucet somewhere in the house. Each pipe has a handle on it to shut off the flow of water. Turn off the flow of cold water into the tank. Leave the hot water pipe alone.

If you have a gas heater, look on the side of the water heater for a squarish box with a temperature dial on the side of it and one or two buttons on top of it. The box may be located near the floor or at eye level. If may also have a removable protective shell over it.

The typical control box has, as mentioned, a temperature dial (see sketch B), a red button used for reigniting the pilot light when it is out and another dial with the words on, off and pilot printed on it. It's the "on-off-pilot" switch that you're interested in at this point.

Turn the dial to "pilot" (do not pass "off" in the process or you will extinguish the pilot light). This keeps the gas burner from coming on while you are draining the tank.

Electric water heaters usually have switches located on the house wall near the water heater or near the household fuse box. They look like ordinary light switches. There may be one or two. Turn them both off.

Draining the water heater will be much easier if you open a hot water faucet somewhere in the house—preferably upstairs. This allows air to replace the water that is leaving the tank.

Get a length of garden hose to attach to the drain valve. You will be dealing with quite a bit of water and an ordinary bucket just won't be satisfactory. Drain valves vary somewhat in style, but most are made to take a garden hose connection. Run the hose to the basement floor drain, or out the door. Try to keep the end of the hose low. Water in the tank will drain to a level no lower than the end of the hose.

The drain valve itself should be on the side of the water heater, near the floor. It usually looks just like an outdoor water hydrant (see sketch A). Turn it to the open position and let all of the water leave the tank.

The bottom of the water tank inside the water heater is dome shaped (as in sketch A), allowing sediment to collect in the low places beneath the level of the drain valve. It's no great tragedy if that sediment never gets entirely cleared out.

But you can get rid of some of it by the following steps: After all the water is drained from the tank,

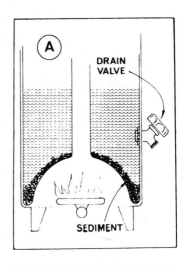

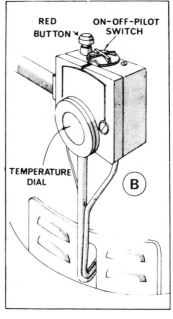

turn on the cold water inlet valve on the pipe at the top of the water heater. Turn it on full blast to stir up any loose sediment in the bottom of the tank. Let it run just until water is coming out strongly from the drain valve, then shut it off and let the tank drain down again. Do this two or three times until the draining water runs fairly clear.

When the job is finished, shut the drain valve. Turn on the cold water inlet valve and leave it on. Go upstairs to the hot water faucet that you left open; wait until water starts coming out of it and then close it. Go to each additional hot water faucet in the house, turn it on until water comes out and then shut it. This removes air from the system.

Finally, return to the water heater and turn the on-off-pilot dial back to "on" (or flip the electric switches).

33/ Keep portable humidifier clean

Portable humidifiers do not require much attention. But an occasional cleaning will keep the device adding moisture to the house efficiently.

The most common design for portable humidifiers is a rotating drum covered with a removable strip of foam. The drum turns—much like a mill wheel—through a pan of water at the bottom of the humidifier.

A small fan then sends the moisture collected in the foam out into the air.

When the foam strip around the drum gets caked with mineral deposits, it does not function properly. The strip should therefore be kept reasonably clean and pliable.

Manufacturers recommend replacing the foam (available at heating-cooling supply stores) once a year. You can also remove the strips periodically and wash them in mild detergent or a baking soda solution.

To do this, it is often easiest to remove the entire drum. Different manufacturers give different in-

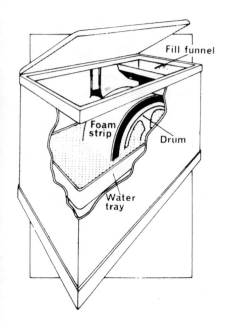

Foam strip

Fill funnel

Drum

Water tray

structions. But in many cases the drum simply lifts off the wheel-like braces on which it rests. Unplug the unit before removing the drum.

You should also clean the water tray occasionally to get rid of mineral deposits and stale water. Unplug the unit and check the back side of it for a removable panel that will give easy access to the water tray.

There are liquid chemicals on the market (from humidifier dealers) that can be added to the humidifier's water to inhibit mineral and bacteria formations. But even with these chemicals, the unit should be cleaned and freshened at least once or twice each year.

HERE'S HOW TO:

34/ Wash draperies in your own home

You can wash draperies in your own home just like professionals do it in a shop. The only requirements are these:

You must know the fabric of your drapes, whether washable or not. And you need a sturdy clothesline, preferably outdoors.

Fabrics that must be dry cleaned should naturally not be washed. Also steer away from washing fab-

ric-lined drapes (the lining may shrink) or pure cotton or antique satin drapes. They also will shrink unless guaranteed preshrunk at the time of purchase.

But synthetics usually wash well, as do sheers. If, after all precautions, your drapes do shrink, a professional cleaner can usually stretch them back again.

Dab some warm water and detergent on the back side of the drapery hem to test for color fastness. Blot the spot with a white cloth. If the color bleeds, better forget doing the drapes yourself.

Once you have determined that the wash job can be done, fill a smooth tub (the bathtub is good) with water and laundry detergent at about bath temperature—warm, not hot. Make the detergent mixture mild to moderate; a low sudsing detergent is best.

Remove the drapes from the traverse rod, but leave the hooks

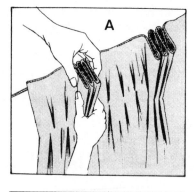

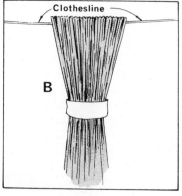

on the drapes. You'll need them again soon and they won't get in your way during washing.

Wash drapes in pairs so that one curtain won't get any cleaner than its mate. Press the drapes down into the soapy water, putting the drapery-hook end of one curtain at the opposite end of the tub from the other. Do not scrub the drapes, but agitate them gently up and down in the water. A plunger or "plumber's helper" is a good prod and will save your back.

The whole point of this project is to be gentle. The sun often weakens drapery fabric. Machine washing and drying is harder on weak fabric than hand treatment is.

After about 15 minutes of soaking and agitating the drapes, it is time to rinse them. Do not wring the fabric out before rinsing.

Instead, lift the drapes up and let some of the soapy water drain out of them. Then transfer them straight to a sturdy clothesline or wire, hanging the drapes by their hooks just as they would hang at a window, spread fully.

The next step is to bring out the garden hose. This is why you need an outdoor clothesline or one over a basement floor drain. Spray the drapes with the hose to rinse.

Use a moderate spray (too hard may damage the fabric) and start at the top, giving special attention to the "header" or top hem. Work the spray on down the length of the drapes on both sides, making sure all soap is flushed away.

Let the drapes drip dry on the line, hung just as they are. You can help keep the permanent pleats in the header from losing their form. Fold the pleats into proper shape. Hold them at the top with one hand. With the other hand, strip the water out of them with a downward motion (see sketch A). Don't go past the header into the main portion of the drape. You can pin the header pleats to shape if you want. But this will slow down the drying process and may leave a crease.

When the drapes are dry, reinforce the header pleats with an iron heated to a temperature appropriate for the fabric; also touch up the rest of the drapery quickly if needed.

Most drapes are supposed to have easy, rounded pleats down the body. You can't get this effect with an iron.

After pressing the drapes, hang them by the hooks again—either on a line or at the window. Gather them into accordian pleats by hand and staple or tape wide strips of paper or cloth around the drapes at intervals of a foot or two (see sketch B). Leave them that way for about a day.

Sheers should be washed the same way as regular drapes. But most sheers do not have drapery hooks. So when it comes time to rinse, spread the sheers out full over two strands of clothesline.

Caution: If you wash fiberglass drapes, be sure to clean the tub out well afterward. These curtains leave a thin film of glass particles in the tub. The particles are irritating to skin, so wash your hands well too after doing the drapes.

35/ Remove candle wax

Candlelight dinners are very romantic—sometimes even essential during power outages.

But the atmosphere loses something when you discover the next morning that candle wax has globbed itself all over your table-cloth, good buffet or mantlepiece.

To remove candle wax from cloth, break as much of the cooled wax off the surface of the cloth as possible.

Place the stained portion of cloth between two pieces of

blotter paper and press with a warm, dry iron (see sketch). Thick paper toweling can substitute for blotter paper. Move the paper or

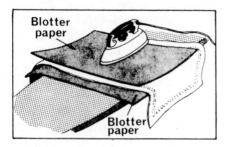

use fresh pieces often as the wax is absorbed into it.

Another method, if the fabric will stand it, is to pour boiling water through the wax stain, melting it out.

The final traces of wax can often be removed with dry cleaning fluid. If you have used the boiling water treatment, let the fabric dry before applying the fluid.

Most modern furniture has a fairly rugged varnish finish. So candle wax itself should not wreak much havoc. Any damage is more likely to happen while you are trying to get the stuff off.

To make the job easier make sure the wax is as hard as possible. Run an ice cube over it. If it is soft you will just smear it around.

If there is a big pile of wax, you can scrape the worse of it away with a dull knife. But as you approach the surface of the table, it is better to switch instruments.

A popsicle stick (or a tongue depressor, if you happen to be a nurse) is a good choice. The wood is soft enough to minimize any possibility of scratching the table. Those stir sticks given out by paint stores are also useful.

You can make the scraper more effective by sanding the end to a spatula-like edge.

Remove the last traces of wax with a piece of clean cheese cloth and a couple drops of lighter fluid or cleaning fluid. Turn the cloth often and confine your efforts to the stained area.

Follow up with furniture polish or paste wax. Treatment of painted furniture is the same. But if the paint job in in poor condition, there may be no way to avoid damaging it slightly.

36/ Keep wood from turning to dust while sawing

It's fine to read about easy build-it-yourself projects like bookcases and tables. But all involve sawing wood.

If you're an amateur at this sort of thing, the simple job of sawing often turns out to be so discouraging that the whole project is scrapped—just like the lumber you've chewed up.

The most common types of hand saws are crosscut and rip saws. A crosscut is designed for cutting across the grain of a board; a rip saw is designed for cutting with the grain. If you don't know what your saw is, it is probably crosscut. It is the most common and useful. If you are getting ready to buy a saw, an eight point crosscut will be a good all-purpose one. (Eight point means there are eight teeth to the inch.)

A crosscut saw can be used to rip. But not vice versa.

First of all a saw should be sharp. If you suspect it isn't, have a professional sharpen it.

Mark your prospective path with a pencil. To begin your cut, brace the saw blade with the thumb of your free hand (carefully) and draw the saw up toward you a couple of times to just make a nick in the wood. Now you are ready to work in earnest.

Hold the saw at about a 45-degree angle to the wood. Grip the handle firmly, extending your forefinger along the handle as a sort of guide or brace.

Most beginners make the mistake of trying to cut with both strokes of the saw. Cutting should be done only on the down or push stroke. The up or pull stroke is just to get the saw back in position. Do not bear down on the saw when cutting. Just push it and let the weight of the saw itself do most of the work. On the up stroke, you can even lift slightly.

Make long strokes, using as much of the blade as possible.

After you get a good distance into the wood, the saw may begin

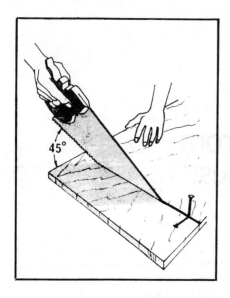

"binding" and you will have trouble moving the blade. This is because the wood is closing in on itself after the cut and holding the saw blade like a vise. The remedy is simple. Insert a nail or a small wedge of wood into the cut (as shown in sketch). Move the nail toward you gradually as you get deeper into the wood.

If you wander off of the pencil mark you have drawn, take the saw blade back to the point where you deviated. Take short strokes along the line until you are back on the track. This is easier than trying to "bend" back into the proper cutting line from somewhere outside it.

HERE'S HOW TO:

37/ Get the best use out of your drill

It's hard to do much of anything constructive around the house without a drill.

Most people who confine themselves to odd jobs around the house have either a small electric drill or a hand crank drill (it has a little wheel you turn, sort of like a hand egg beater).

Any decent hardware store has a whole rack full of drill bits (the removable rod that actually does the drilling). Different sizes, different purposes and shapes. What do you need? What does it look like?

There are three things you need to know upon entering the store: The size of the chuck on your drill (explanation to follow), the size of the hole you want to drill and the type of material you will be working on.

Most hand drills are 1/4-inch drills. This means the chuck (the nose opening where you insert the bit) will accept nothing larger than 1/4 inch in diameter. It will, however, close down to accept anything smaller.

Inexpensive electric drills are mostly either 1/4 or 3/8-inch drills (again, referring to the chuck size). They have an advantage over hand drills in that they provide more muscle and can be adapted as sanders and buffers with special attachments.

If you have a hand crank drill, you need an assortment of ordin-

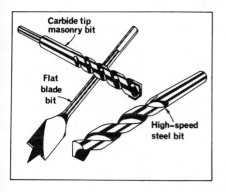

Carbide tip masonry bit

Flat blade bit

High–speed steel bit

ary high-speed steel bits (see sketch). They can be bought singly or in sets that drill holes anywhere from 1/16 of an inch to 1/4 inch. If you are drilling a hole larger than 1/4 inch, you can get a larger bit that has a shank or stem that is cut down to fit into a 1/4-inch chuck.

The very cheapest bit sets are

made of carbon steel and will drill wood easily. But it is smarter to invest a couple of dollars more and get high-speed steel bits. They will handle wood, thin sheet metal (like kitchen cabinets), plaster and plastic. This is all you really need with a hand crank drill, since you can't get enough leverage to drill concrete or masonry with it anyway.

The same basic kind of high-speed steel bit set should be bought for a light-duty electric drill. But in addition, there are a couple of extra options because of the higher turning power of the electric.

One of these is a flat-blade bit (see sketch). It is meant for drilling wood only and should be your choice if you are drilling any hole larger than 1/4 inch in wood. The reason is that a flat-blade bit is cheaper (past 1/4 inch) than a spiral bit of the same diameter.

The other bit that you will probably buy eventually is a carbide-tipped bit for masonry, brick and concrete. This kind of bit looks much like the plain spiral bit for wood and metal. But the tip of it has a wedge inserted into it that looks almost like an afterthought (see sketch).

Some masonry bits are slightly more expensive than plain bits and should be bought singly after you determine how large a hole you want to drill. Like the larger diameter wood and steel bits, they are available with cut-down shanks so they will fit into the drill.

38/ Make drilling easier

There's something very frustrating about watching a person drill into a wall or door frame, get the drill bit stuck in there and then try to get it out. The person in question usually pulls and tugs at the drill until it suddenly comes loose and he flies across the room—or until the drill bit breaks.

It's frustrating to watch because the remedy is so simple. If you are using a small hand crank drill (the kind that looks sort of like a heavy-duty egg beater), you simply turn the crank wheel in the opposite direction, reversing the action of the drill bit. It is then easy to back the bit out of the hole.

If you are using a hand electric drill, it may or may not have a reverse button on it. Many simple models don't. But just give the drill

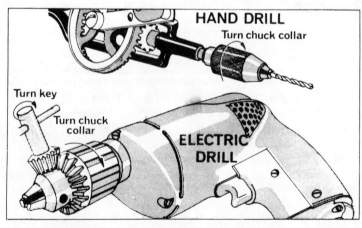

HAND DRILL
Turn chuck collar

Turn key
Turn chuck collar

ELECTRIC DRILL

a little spurt of power in the regular forward direction while pulling the drill back at the same time.

You ought to pull a drill out of its hole every now and then anyway if you are drilling anything an inch or deeper. (Keep the drill turning as you pull it out.) The reason is to clear the hole of chips and debris. These chips not only make drilling harder, they can even enlarge the hole in some cases.

There are other handy things to know about drilling. For instance, you really should have a gismo called a center punch. This is sort of like a fat nail or spike that you smack with a hammer to make an initial hole or dent in either metal or wood. Center punches are available at hardware stores, often for less than a dollar. The purpose of the hole or dent is to give the drill bit something to home in on until it bites into the material.

Unless you need to drill a hole at an odd angle, a drill should be held at a 90-degree angle to your work. And don't press too hard. Just keep moderate pressure on the drill and let the bit set its own pace through the material. This is especially true with a small electric drill, which can overheat if you strain it.

(The exception is in drilling masonry with a carbide tip, where you press hard and turn the drill slowly. An electric drill with variable speeds is best for this. If your electric has just one speed, be careful of burning it out on masonry.)

Are you an amateur who has inherited a used drill without directions? Then you'll need to know how to change the drill bits.

The business end of a drill—the part that holds the drill bits secure—is called a chuck. It expands and contracts to hold bits of various diameters (although small hand drills don't usually expand to more than 1/4 or 3/8 inch).

The chuck on a hand crank drill is very simple to operate. Hold the crank wheel and body of the drill firmly with one hand to keep the wheel from turning. With the other hand, rotate the metal collar of the chuck counterclockwise to loosen, clockwise to tighten (see sketch).

The metal collar of the chuck on an electric drill also turns. But there is an additional securing mechanism because of the higher speed of the electric drill.

Just in front of the collar on the electric chuck you will see three holes. There should also be, with the drill, a metal "key"—sort of an exaggerated version of a skate key (see sketch).

Insert the key into one of the holes and turn it counterclockwise to loosen the jaws of the chuck. Then turn the chuck collar to the diameter you want. Insert the new drill bit. Close down the chuck collar and tighten the loosened jaws with the key. (Not too tight. You won't get it undone again.)

Don't change bits while an electric drill is plugged in. You could chew up a finger.

39/ Solder - a handy talent to have around the house

Being able to solder may not sound like the most glamorous claim in the world.

But a rudimentary knowledge of soldering can come in very handy for lots of small repair chores around the house. You can often fix broken jewelry, fill a hole in a metal pail or fuse the stranded ends of an electrical wire with a drop of solder.

There are different kinds of solder and soldering irons. But the amateur repairman doesn't need to know about all of them.

Two general-purpose solders that are easy to use are acid-core solder and rosin-core solder. They both look like hefty wire and come wound on spools. Both contain a central core of material that acts as a "flux"—a cleaning and bonding agent. (Plain solder without a core requires application of a separate flux to the material being worked on.)

If you have to choose just one solder to keep around home, rosin core is probably your best choice. It can be used on both ferrous and nonferrous metals (either jewelry, wires or metal pails). Acid core works well on ferrous metals (those containing a portion of iron). But the work must be washed well after soldering or else the acid of the core will start corroding the metal. This makes acid core impractical for electrical connections and for some jewelry.

You can forget about trying to solder stainless steel, aluminum or chromium. They take special fluxes and solders and are too difficult for the novice.

Solder is made from tin and lead. Good quality solders that melt fast have a ratio of about 60 per cent tin to 40 per cent lead. The higher the lead content, the harder it is to melt the solder.

Home soldering irons are of two general types. One is the kind that looks like a fat screwdriver with a cord on the end of it. The other is a soldering gun, which looks like a pistol with a couple or sturdy wires in place of the barrel. It works with a trigger.

The rod irons are commonly available for home use from 30 watts to 100 watts in capacity.

They all get hot enough for soldering. But the larger the iron, the larger its heat output and the larger the soldering job you can do.

Soldering guns have the advantage of heating up much faster than soldering irons. But many models continue to heat as long as you hold the trigger down, and you can melt the piece you are working on.

There are two basic rules for soldering.

First: the metal to be worked on must be free of paint and absolutely clean. Use a scouring soap pad on it, then rinse and dry. Or use steel wool and dry cleaning fluid. There can be no oil or dirt on the metal at all. That means keeping your fingers off the cleaned surface.

Second: The material to be repaired is your melting medium—not the soldering iron. This means that the iron is really used only to heat the material being worked on. The heated material then melts the solder. Solder applied to cold metal will not adhere.

Before beginning to solder, you must "tin" the end of your soldering iron. Tinning is simply coating the tapered point of the iron with solder. This makes the iron transfer heat more efficiently to the piece you're working on.

Don't try to tin the iron after it is red hot. The solder will just bead and make a big mess. Instead, hold a piece of wire solder against the end of the iron as the iron heats (see sketch A). When the solder begins to melt, spread it around over the whole tip of the iron. The iron has now reached the proper temperature for work.

Put the piece of metal you're working on in some kind of vise. If you have a metal shop vise, fine. If not, put your clever brain to work. Wooden clothespins make good clamps for holding small objects.

Even if you have a metal vise available, it is a good idea to place thin pieces of wood or asbestos shingling between the vise edges and the metal you're working on. This keeps the heat from spreading out and being partially lost in the metal of the vise.

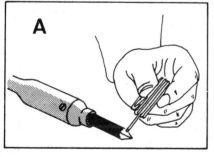

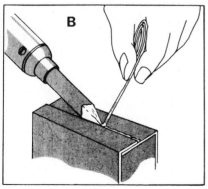

If you are mending a cracked piece of metal, place the two cracked edges as close together as possible. Then lay one tapered, tinned angle of the soldering iron on the crack to heat the working surface.

Touch the soldering wire to the heated crack, just in front of the iron's point. When the temperature of the working surface gets high enough, the solder will melt into and over the crack.

Move the soldering iron slowly on down the crack following it with the solder wire (see sketch B). At no time do you try to melt the solder onto your work by placing the wire under the end of the iron. Let the heated work surface do the melting job.

When dealing with something intricate like a cufflink or a piece of jewelry, you probably will not have a nice straight crack to work on.

In cases where the soldering iron won't reach both surfaces to be joined, try "tinning" both surfaces.

Then place the two tinned surfaces face to face and use the soldering iron to heat the larger of the two pieces (or the easier to deal with). Keep the iron as close to the area to be joined as possible. As the larger piece reaches temperature, the two tinned surfaces should join satisfactorily.

Beginners shouldn't try soldering really valuable jewelry. And before you work on anything, try your skill on pieces of scrap metal.

HERE'S HOW TO:

40/ Cope when the electrical power fails

Severe thunderstorms and flooding seem to make themselves right at home every now and then—your home, that is.

There are a few things you should do when these unwelcome guests arrive.

If you suddenly lose all electrical power in your house, check to see if your neighbors have the same problem. If they don't, you have undoubtedly blown a main fuse and should call the electrical company.

If several houses or the whole area is in darkness, there may be a line down somewhere and you should still call the company.

Whichever the case, your next step should be to unplug all motor-driven appliances that normally run constantly. This means the refrigerator, the freezer, air conditioning units and anything else you can think of that might turn on automatically when the power returns.

There are two reasons for this. First, it takes more energy to start a motor than to keep it running. If all motors in your house start at one time when the electricity returns, you are likely to blow a fuse.

Second, power occasionally does not come back on at full voltage. Motors that run—or try to run—on reduced voltage soon burn themselves out.

Do leave a couple of light switches on so you can tell when you have electricity again.

The rule about unplugging motor-driven appliances also holds during "brown-outs" when the electric company reduces its voltage or the voltage lowers for some other reason.

Signs of lowered voltage are dimming light bulbs, a flopping and shrinking television picture, motors that hum but won't start (turn them off right away), or fluorescent lights that start blinking (turn them off too).

If your basement is flooded, do not step into the water if the water is in contact with any electrically energized appliance—this means anything that is running or might start running on its own. To do so is to risk your life.

This rule also applies when the water level reaches electrical outlets (they are themselves energized) or plugged-in extension cords. And it makes no difference whether the power is off in your neighborhood. You never know when it will come back on.

Don't touch fuses or circuit breakers while standing in water.

If your basement floods regularly, put your appliances up on risers permanently. Once an appliance has been soaked, wait about a week before using it to give it time to dry out completely.

41/ Check for proper electrical grounding

Many of today's hand-held tools and major appliances come equipped with three-prong plugs. Hedge clippers, portable dishwashers and garbage disposal units are examples.

The third prong is a "grounding" device. This means that in case of a short in the appliance, the "ground" is designed to direct wandering electrical impulses away from you and back into the electrical outlet box.

In houses built within the past six or eight years, all electrical outlets are made to take three-prong plugs. This is a nationwide standard.

But with older houses, chances are you will have to trip off to the dime store for an adapter (see sketch A) before you can plug in a three-prong appliance.

These adapters cost under a dollar and plug right into your wall outlet. Branching off from the adapter is a short wire or "pigtail" with a metal hook on the end of it. The hook is to be fastened under the center screw of the outlet plate (as shown in sketch A). There are directions included with the adapter.

This procedure supposedly completes your grounding path. (The center screw on the outlet plate is connected to the outlet box, which is supposed to be grounded.)

But there's a catch.

Not all boxes for the old-fashioned, two-prong outlets are in fact grounded. And there's no way to tell by looking.

There is a simple test to find out. It requires an investment of under a dollar.

First, visit a hardware store and buy what is called a pigtail light socket. This is a simple light socket with two wires coming out the back of it instead of two prongs. (See sketch B.)

Screw a regular light bulb (25 watt is plenty) into the socket. Now examine the two wires. They should be covered with rubberized insulation except for about an inch of bare stranded wire at the ends.

Just above the bare wire, wrap a wad of electrician's tape around the insulation for a firmer hand-hold on the wire (see sketch B).

When performing this test, do not hold onto anything metal and do not touch the bare strands of wire.

Look closely at the wall outlet you are preparing to test. On nearly every outlet manufactured during the last 50 years, one prong hole is shorter and skinnier than the other.

Stick one of the bare light socket wires into the short skinny hole. Wriggle it around a bit to make good contact.

Touch the other bare wire to the center screw of the outlet plate.

The bulb will light up if your electrical box is grounded.

(You can run the same test on newer three-prong outlets, using the rounded grounding hole instead of the plate screw.)

But don't give up testing just yet. If the bulb does not light, change the one bare light bulb wire from the skinny prong hole to the fatter prong hole. (The other wire

still touches the outlet screw.)

If the bulb lights this way, it is good news and bad news. The electrical box is grounded all right. But the "polarity" of your outlet is backward.

Reversed polarity is too complicated to explain here except to say that it is dangerous. If an appliance with a polarized plug is used on an outlet with reversed polarity, you have a good chance of electric shock.

One such outlet means all the outlets in the house should be checked. A few final words about grounding. A lack of it should be remedied by an experienced elec-

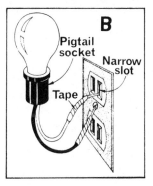

B

Pigtail socket

Narrow slot

Tape

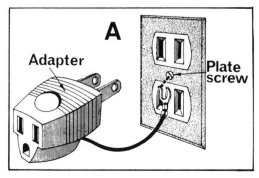

A

Adapter

Plate screw

trician—as should the problem of reversed polarity.

Some hand-held tools need no grounding because they are double insulated. They are usually marked with a statement on the name plate and/or an international symbol—a small square within a larger one.

Many other two-prong appliances, like toasters, are not double insulated and are not grounded. They should be disconnected when not in use. Plugging a two-prong appliance into a three-prong adapter does nothing to ground the appliance.

Never circumvent grounding devices or instructions when they are provided—especially on camper trailers or swimming pool pumps.

HERE'S HOW TO:

42/ Repair a pull chain on a light fixture

A light with a pull chain that won't work every time is enough to make you want to yank the fixture out whole.

As a matter of fact, that's just about what you'll end up doing to fix it—but not in blind rage.

When a pull chain doesn't work, there is usually something amiss inside the socket. It's not really possible to repair it. You'll need to replace it—a job that is not expensive or particularly difficult if you take it step by step.

Let's assume your pull-chain light is a hanging fixture. (If it's a table lamp just turn the accompanying sketch upside down.)

The light bulb screws into a socket which is covered by a metal shell. The shell, in turn, snaps into a half-round metal cap of the same color (see sketch). The electrical wires from the ceiling feed down through a hole in the top of this cap.

The first thing you want to do is shut off the electricity to the light fixture you'll be working on. Do this by unscrewing the fuse or flipping the circuit breaker that controls electricity to that part of the house.

Unscrew the light bulb from its socket.

The next step is to separate the

metallic shell from its cap. Most shells snap into place under the cap and have a spot on the body of the shell where the words "press here" are printed. (If you don't see this, the shell may be held to the cap by a band or ring that unscrews.)

The people who designed the snap-in shells never meant for anyone but Hercules to unfasten the devices. When you "press here," you will likely get no results. An easier way is to get a very thin screwdriver, slip it up under the edge of the cap and pry gently at several different points while pulling down on the shell. Start at the "press" sign.

This method risks bending the cap out of shape, so take it easy and don't rush.

As you pull the shell away, you will expose a small, rectangular gismo with one screw on each side of it. This is the combination socket and switch. The screws are called terminal screws and the two electrical wires from the ceiling will be attached to them. Remove the wires by loosening the terminal screws.

Since you will not be replacing the metal cap of the light fixture, don't try to remove it. Just leave it where it is.

Take the metal shell and the faulty socket with you to a hardware or dime store and have them matched for size and type. You usually have to buy the new switch-socket with a new shell around it. They come as a unit.

(Inside the new shell will be a cardboard liner. Don't throw it away. Leave it in there when installing the new socket.)

Back home again, take the new socket mechanism out of its shell and attach the electrical wires to the terminal screws. Use the same two wires that were attached to the old socket.

One terminal screw on the new

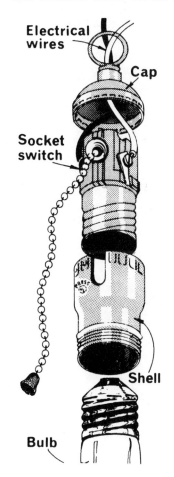

Electrical wires

Cap

Socket switch

Shell

Bulb

socket will be brass colored; the other silver. If one of the electrical wires you are working with is white and the other black, run the white wire to the silver screw and the black wire to the brass screw. Light to light; dark to dark. (In fact if one of the wires has any identifying marks at all—like a colored thread in the covering—it should go to the white terminal screw.)

If both electrical wires are identical, it doesn't matter which one goes to which screw.

Make a three-quarter loop at the end of each wire and hook the end of the wire under its appropriate terminal screw. Turn the screw down tight. If the bare wire end is stranded, make sure there are no strands bristling out from under the terminal screw.

Once the wires are secured, slip the shell back up over the new socket and snap the shell firmly into the metal cap. It usually clicks twice.

Replace the light bulb, turn on the electricity to that part of the house and try your new light fixture.

43/ Install a wall dimmer switch

Dimmer switches can allow you to create a lot of different effects in your home with lighting. And there's no special trick to installing the switches.

Dimmer switches work with regular light bulbs. But there are a couple of things to keep in mind before installing the switch.

The first is to buy one that has been tested and rated for watt capacity. The watt capacity of the dimmer switch must exceed the to-

tal wattage of the light bulb (or bulbs) to be used with it.

The second point is to make sure the light switch you are replacing does not control some appliance outlet as well as the light you have in mind.

Now to installation.

Begin by shutting off the electricity to the wall switch you'll be working on. Do this by removing the proper fuse in the household fusebox or by flipping the circuit

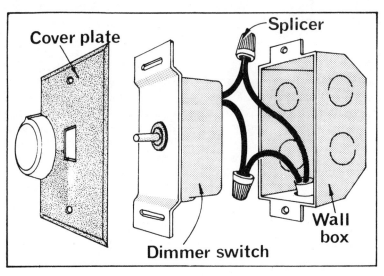

Cover plate

Splicer

Dimmer switch

Wall box

breaker switch.

Unfasten the screws holding the wall plate or cover on the old light switch. You should now see the switch mechanism sitting in an open-sided box inserted in the wall.

The switch is usually held in place by two screws running into the front edge of the wall box. Undo these and pull the switch forward.

You should now see two wires connected to the switch. If there are more than two, you've got something more complicated than a single-pole switch and these instructions will not apply.

To remove the old switch, look for two screws on the switch body holding the ends of the wires. Loosen the screws and unhook the wires.

On some light switches, the wires don't run to screws. Instead, they feed into little holes in the back of the switch body. Internal clamps hold them secure. To release the clamps, look for a small hole with "Press Here" or something similar written above it. Inserting a miniature screwdriver into the hole will release the clamp.

The new dimmer switch, if it is a common type, will have two wires of its own running out the back of it. These are to be hooked to the two wall wires that were attached to the old switch.

It doesn't really matter which switch wire is attached to which wall wire. (One wall wire may be black and the other white; or both may be black. Just use whatever was used on the other switch.)

Included in the package with your dimmer switch, you will often find two little plastic things that resemble sewing thimbles. These are splicers and are to be used for connecting the wire ends together.

Hold the exposed end of one switch wire and the end of one wall wire together side by side. Then screw the splicer cap down over the two ends. Turn the splicer until it's secure, but don't overdo.

One important thing to watch: The bottom edge of the splicer cap should come down well over the insulated portion of the two wires. If there is exposed wire showing, unscrew the splicer and clip the wire ends to a length that will fit within the cap.

With both connections completed, stuff the spliced wires to the back of the wall box, slide the dimmer switch into place and secure it with screws.

44/ Treat a power mower

Every summer adults and children are injured by rotary power mowers—usually through carelessness.

Cutting blades are not the only danger—stones, glass and other debris can be hurled many feet by a rotary mower—with deadly effect.

Make sure you aren't involved in a mower accident this year—follow these safety rules:

Know your controls; read the owner's manual carefully and learn how to stop the mower engine quickly in an emergency.

Keep children and pets as far away from the mower as possible.

Disengage all blade and drive gears before starting (on units so equipped). Start the engine carefully with feet well away from the blades.

Check all nuts, bolts and screws often to be sure the mower is in safe operating condition.

Do not operate the engine where carbon monoxide fumes can collect.

Never cut grass by pulling the mower toward you.

Be extremely careful when using a riding mower on slopes. It can turn over.

Make sure the lawn is clear of sticks, stones, wire and other debris.

Do not overspeed the engine or alter governor settings. High speed is dangerous and shortens mower life.

Never leave inertia-type starters in a wound-up position.

Stop engine and disconnect spark plug wire before checking or working on the mower.

Add fuel before starting the engine—never while the engine is running.

Do not allow anyone to operate mower without instructions.

Stop the engine before pushing mower across gravel drives or walks. Also stop it whenever you leave the mower, even for a moment.

Don't drive too close to creek or ditch edges and watch out for traffic when near roads.

Stay alert for holes and other hidden hazards.

Keep all shields and safety devices in place.

Do not carry passengers on a riding mower.

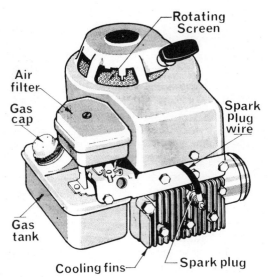

Rotating Screen

Air filter

Gas cap

Spark Plug wire

Gas tank

Cooling fins

Spark plug

45/ Keep a power mower working properly

Power lawn mowers are only used six months out of the year, and often they don't get proper maintenance during the lawn-mowing season. Why not check your power mower now, before the day of reckoning comes along and you find the blankety-blank thing won't start?

Before doing any cleaning or checking, make sure all mower switches are turned off and the spark wire is disconnected. Otherwise the blades might give a turn or two unexpectedly.

The spark wire? This is a little electric cord that hooks to the top of the spark plug which, in turn, fires the engine. Motor styles vary from size to size and maker to maker. But the spark wire (and top end of the spark plug) are generally somewhere on the outside of the motor, accessible without taking the housing apart. The Briggs & Stratton motor shown in the sketch is an example.

Spark wires sometimes just clip or slide into place over the plug end; others are held in place with a screw.

While in the neighborhood, you

93

might as well check the spark plug. It unscrews. There is usually a copper gasket or washer around the screw-threads of the spark plug; be sure not to lose it, as it is necessary for a proper fit.

At the threaded end of the spark plug are two little metal points across which the spark is supposed to jump (see sketch). These should be free of all carbon and corrosion. Scrape gently to clean. Look carefully at the two points; they should have nice straight edges and squared-off ends. If they are jagged, the plug probably needs to be replaced (not expensive) with the same style plug.

Try not to widen the gap between the points while cleaning; it's hard to set right again without a specially-made measuring tool. If for some reason you have further separated the points, however, the thickness of a dime will approximate what the measure should be.

Clean dust, dirt and grass clippings from cutting blades and from the rotating screen and cooling system (this should be done after each use).

The air filter should be cleaned or replaced. A common type of filter used today is a piece of foam rubber-like material contained in a small metal box closed with a nut and bolt. Remove the foam; squeeze it out in a container of kerosene. Dry the foam by squeezing it in a cloth; then soak it with engine oil, squeezing it once more

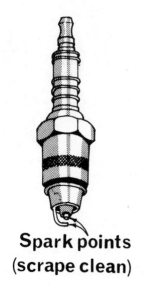

Spark points (scrape clean)

to remove excess oil and replace in its box.

Air filters are found in various places, but should be marked on the mower itself. Clean or replace for every 25 hours of operation or according to owner's manual directions.

Lubricate the wheels by putting a few drops of oil where the axle sticks through the hub of the wheel (some wheels have a little hole in the hub for adding a few drops).

Cutting blades should be well sharpened. They can be unbolted with an adjustable wrench and either sharpened at home (with a 10-inch heavy file or a grinding wheel) or taken to a shop, where the job is quickly done for a small fee.

The height of the blades can be adjusted on many mowers by moving little levers located at each wheel to raise or lower the whole mower.

Check the air vent of the gasoline tank (air has to get into the tank as gas flows out). Some mowers have a little hole in the gas cap, some have a tiny cap on top of the main cap. If your style is the latter, the small cap has to be loose while the mower is running. In either case, swizzle the gas cap around in a container of kerosene to loosen dust and dirt in the vent.

Some mowers have what's called a settling bowl—a little glass or clear plastic cup set into the fuel line between the gas tank and the motor to catch gunk in the gasoline. The settling bowl should be removed and cleaned with kerosene. But FIRST close the gas line shut-off valve (usually a little butterfly or wing nut) on the fuel line at the bottom of the gas tank.

There are two basic types of power mower engines—four-stroke and two-stroke engines. No need here to explain the differences except to say that a four-stroke generally uses straight gasoline and has a special crankcase or sump for motor oil. (Oil should be drained and changed once every 25 hours of operation or sooner if owner's booklet so states.)

With two-stroke engines, on the other hand, the lubricating oil is usually mixed with the gasoline right in the fuel tank. The point is—if your mower is a two-stroke, you should not add raw gasoline to the tank. The gas should be mixed with motor oil in a ratio specified in the owner's booklet. (If, however, you have lost the booklet, a backyard rule is half a pint of oil for every gallon of gas.)